LEN BERGANTINO, Ed.D., Ph.D., A.B.P.P.
Psychoanalysis
(310) 207-9397

Clinical Psychologist
License Number 3837

A.B.P.P. - Diplomate in Family Psychology
American Board of Professional Psychology

Dr. Len Bergantino is the most gifted psychoanalyst whoever lived. Admittedly he had a direct connection with God and the full body of his writings and intended to be "The —Thing—In—Itself" and over the next couple of hundred years evoke an upward spiraling society as opposed to the downward spiraling society form which mankind suffers. These books provide the tools with which to carry on the work of attaining closer and closer approximations of pure being, while at the same time giving psychoanalysis and the world at large a fighting chance against Evil. In direct revelation, God informed me that 12 out of 100,000,000 people cross the pearly gates of Heaven. Doubting Thomases go straight to hell!!!

1215 Brockton Ave., Ste. I04, W. Los Angeles, CA 90025 - U.S.A.

DR. LEN BERGANTINO - CLINICAL PSYCHOLOGY
Diplomate in Family Psychology
American Board of Professional Psychology
Trained by Carl Whitaker, M.D. in Telephonic Family Therapy

TO HIRE ME AS A CONSULTANT
CALL (424) 293-6511
(7 RINGS)

January 9, 2019

MEMO TO C.E.O.
AMERICAN BOARD OF PROFESSIONAL PSYCHOLOGY

Dear President of ABPP:

This letter does not require a response from you to me. It is merely a suggestion as to how YOU OUGHT TO RUN THE ENTIRE FIELD OF PSYCHOLOGY:

1. Do away with all boards of Psychology on a national basis.

2. Over my 42 years in private practice they have crushed any possible growth in the field!

3. Let entry level psychologists engage in private practice with no license. In this way SUPPLY AND DEMAND WILL RESOLVE THE ISSUE OF WHO IS ANY GOOD AND/OR WHO WILL SURVIVE IN THE JUNGLE!

4. There will be an occasional idiot that falls through the cracks of having sex with a patient but (that aside) Boards of Psychology are not worth the effort and are a destructive political force!

5. ABPP, after five years in private practice can provide specialty exams that are valid on a national level and can be shown to indicate "Mine is bigger than yours!" FURTHUR, ABPP WHICH I HAVE HAD SINCE 1992 fostered the best in me and both the preparation for the ABPP exam and the examiners provided a high quality of experience that enhanced my training by Carl Whitaker, M.D. and Walter Kempler, M.D. Whitaker trained me in family therapy from 1981 - 1983 and mentored me from 1979-1994. Kempler trained me from 1977-1983 and mentored me from 1973-1986.

6. AS ABPP IS BASED ON ACTUAL WORK SAMPLE VIA VIDEO AN ABPP EXAM SHOULD BE OPEN TO ANY GROUP DEALING WITH FAMILIES, SUCH AS MINISTERS WHO ORDINARILY DEAL WITH FAMILIES DOING FAMILY THERAPY!

REV. DR. LEN BERGANTINO
PRIME MINISTER - UNIV. LIFE CHURCH - WCA
ED.D. (USC - 1971) DOCTOR OF EDUCATION
PH.D. (INT'L COLLEGE - 1977) CLINICAL PSYCH.

cc:

All Long Distance calls for Family Therapy from Hawaii
paid for by Dr. Bergantino.

1215 Brockton Avenue, Suite 104, Los Angeles, California 90025

Colmery-O'Neil
Veterans Administration
Medical Center

Topeka KS 66622

Veterans Administration

1 July 1985

In Reply Refer To:

Len Bergantino, Ed.D., Ph.D.
10266 Kilrenney Avenue
Los Angeles, California 90064

Dear Len:

How nice to receive yours of June 24th, and to learn of your upward spiral! I'm very pleased indeed to believe that my little review of your book has contributed to your success!

Frankly, Len, I have long been eructatively fed up with the sort of territorial cupidities and other evidences of narcissistic nonsensicality so many of the colleagues display. Such antics reveal the essentially limbic nature of people as it comes to be expressed in envies and jealousies to which you allude in your letter. When I read your book I knew at once of your outsider-ism (cf. Colin Wilson's seminal book of the same name—<u>The Outsider</u>) as well as your talent; since I know I <u>am</u> good also, I do not need to do the Big-Daddy-in-Cat-On-A-Hot-Tin-Roof bit, viz., to shit on one's sons out of envy and fear that they will appropriate my penis-cum-wife-cum-everything-else!

I trust your family are in good health. Keep in touch.

Most sincerely,

Donald B. Rinsley, M.D., F.R.S.H. (Lond.)
Associate Chief for Education
Psychiatry Service

Clinical Professor of Psychiatry
University of Kansas School of Medicine
Kansas City

DBR:mtf

Dr. Len Bergantino, A.B.P.P.

THE GOD FATHER OF CLINICAL PSYCHOLOGY

"The Murderers on the Inside Love Me More than the Murderers on the Outside"

RE: front cover of book

Bill Russell, the most dominant person to ever play any professional sport. 11 out of 13 years Boston Celtics (1957-1969)

Alex Bergantino is my son and my best buddy.

Racism has been a sensitive subject for the longest time in America. While talking about racism, most people focus on racist whites who show intolerance towards minorities like black and brown people. Dr. Len Bergantino is here to enlighten readers on reverse racism, which is very much alive across the U.S. Dr. Len Bergantino tells it as it is. He does not mince words, and neither does he sugarcoat situations. He discusses instances where black people in power have been unjust to white people, who they perceive to be beneath them. This book can be overwhelming for some, but the author ensures that his point is made clearly and effectively.

The Denial of Reverse Racism in America is the kind of book you need if you enjoy following current events and watching the political space. Dr. Len Bergantino writes from experience and from observations. I appreciate the author for calling out what is wrong and for promoting unity even when talking about the cracks racism has caused in society. The author writes about the pros of working together as compared to forming separate groups of people. The writing is clear-cut, and the author writes about everything that concerns racism. I like that he also touches on unconventional topics or subjects considered to be taboo in modern society.

The many examples the author gives show that racism is deeply rooted in many parts of America. Dr. Len Bergantino gives multiple examples to support his views and shares tales where racism almost cost him his life. While some pages in this book may be difficult to read, the lessons shared by the author are remarkable. Victim mentality, manipulation, and being mean-spirited are other subjects that the author addresses. The biggest lesson in the book is a line from one of the author's texts 'There are only black and white individuals, do not treat individuals as races.' This line is crucial as it reminds us not to judge others based on their race but rather on their character as individuals. Dr. Len Bergantino, despite having gone through the worst, advocates for harmony and decency.

When a child is born, they do not know color. *The Denial of Reverse Racism in America* will make you wish that everyone treated everyone like children do. Less judgment and more unity. This book is an interesting read, despite having some extreme takes. I recommend *The Denial of Reverse Racism in America* to readers that previously denounced the existence of reverse racism, as the many examples shared by the author will convince you of its existence.

Pages: 84 | ASIN: B0861RZPZZ

THE DENIAL OF REVERSE RACISM IN AMERICA
First Review

The Denial of Reverse Racism in America by Dr. Len Bergantino is an attempt to prove the theory that reverse racism exists and is a serious problem. From the start, the author makes his views clear on the subject, using anecdotal experiences throughout his life as a means to support his argument. He believes his experiences, which include his perspective on programs and organizations attempting to address racial inequality, substantiate his stance, though his argument to support this case comes from deeply held personal beliefs rather than using statistics and research to support the topic.

While this book may be a difficult read for many, it serves as an interesting glimpse into the mind of someone who feels strongly about this topic. Throughout the book, the author references his experiences from childhood, university, and his years working as a school counselor. He frequently uses capitalization to emphasize his points throughout the book, though the overall tone feels intensely emotional and abrupt.

I found the book interesting from a more critical perspective, and how the author eagerly argues the point for reverse racism by mentioning various anecdotal scenarios as proof for this case. While I found it compelling, I would have appreciated more hard evidence to support his views. While the author approaches the topic from a particular viewpoint, he manages to stay with the theme consistently.

The Denial of Reverse Racism in America by Dr. Len Bergantino serves as an intriguing look into the mind and thoughts of someone who strongly believes in the concept of reverse racism. I suggest reading the book, and the author's explanations, as it's like a case study into one individual's views.

Pages: 84 | ASIN: 1648032680

 Xlibris

The Denial of Reverse Racism in America

<u>DECLARATION OF DR. LEN BERGANTINO</u>

I, DR. LEN BERGANTINO, DECLARE:

Bill Russell personally gave me permission to take his picture with my developmentally delayed son Alex Bergantino around the year 2003 when he was making an appearance supporting an orthopaedic pain relief Medical doctor whereby Bill Russell discussed the wear and tear from running up and down hardwood floors on the joints of his body. This meeting and this picture were taken at the sports Club Los Angeles at 7 p.m. in the evening on Westwood Blvd. just south of Santa Monica blvd.

I declare under penalty of perjury that the foregoing is true and correct and I would and could testify as such in a court of law if called upon to do so.

This declaration was written in Los Angeles, California on March 5, 2020.

____

DR. LEN BERGANTINO

The Denial of Reverse
Racism in America

Dr. Len Bergantino, Ed.D., Ph.D.

To order additional copies of this book, contact:
Xlibris
844-714-8691
www.Xlibris.com
Orders@Xlibris.com
810739

ACKNOWLEDGEMENT

XLIBRIS PUBLISHING COMPANY PERSONNEL:

MICHELLE POSTRANO IS A MANAGER WHO GETS THINGS UNSTUCK IN THE MYRIAD OF PLACES THEY CAN GET STUCK AND GETS PROJECTS COMPLETED. BION, THE GREAT BRITISH PSYCHOANALYST SAID "THERE ARE TWO NASTY FACTS. THE FIRST IS THAT PEOPLE NEED TO DEPEND ON OTHER PEOPLE AND THE SECOND IS THAT YOU HAVE TO FIND SOMEONE WHO IS DEPENDWORTHY." MICHELLE POSTRANO IS DEPENDWORTHY.

MONIQUE GOMEZ IS GIFTED. SHE HAS THE ABILITY TO SPEAK TO SOMEONE AND HELP THEM RECOGNIZE THEIR DEEPEST WISH AND THEN PUT THAT WISH INTO PUBLISHING ACTION.

FOR ME PUBLISHING A BOOK IS A NIGHTMARE. MY FIRST BOOK BECAME A MASTER CLASSIC IN THE FIELD IN 1981 -"Psychotherapy, Insight & Style: The Existential Moment, published by Allyn & Bacon, Inc., Boston, 288 pp.) The experience was so torturous that I did not do another book until November 18, 2018. I have done 9 more since then. Xlibris personnel that were helpful in their various company duties and assignments were:

Richard Tecson, Cindy Murray, Carlos Cortes and Joy Daniels.

And of course there was Billy Finn, the greatest basketball player whoever lived, who trained me to become and know enough about basketball to have written this book and to cousin Fred Bredice who could shoot at a level where he hardly ever hit the rim, and only net!

As for the Black Brothers there were many along the way in the fields of sports, music (Miles Davis), education (Lou Thomas), Shirley Jones (co-founder of the Kedren Community Mental Health Center in South

Central Los Angeles, and PSYCHIATRIST PAUL LOGAN, M.D. WHO
GAVE ME A CHANCE WHEN NO ONE ELSE WOULD BECAUSE
HE STATED "I UNDERSTAND BLACK RAGE!"

THE REVEREND DR. LEN BERGANTINO

I have reason to believe that the sum total of characteristics that make up my personality and the variety of occupations, athletics and musical endeavors in which I have engaged provide me with some unique primitive viewpoints regarding racial relations between Blacks and Whites that are and will be worthy of consideration in RACE RELATIONS FOR CENTURIES TO COME.

What makes these comments valuable is the candor with which I report them at the deepest primitive levels, no matter whom they offend, including myself, my parents, my neighbors and in particular not only the Northeast section of the United States but also the West Coast, primarily Los Angeles.

IN OTHER WORDS, IF YOU ARE BORN IN THE UNITED STATES, YOU ARE A RACIST AND IF YOU SAY YOU ARE NOT, YOU ARE A RACIST AND DO NOT KNOW YOU ARE A RACIST! Just as I studied macro-economics in college as opposed to micro-economics, IF ONE EXAMINES THE MINUTIA OF OUR EXPERIENCES IN THE ORDER IN WHICH THEY OCCURRED, WE ARE ALL RACISTS IN AMERICA, TO SOME DEGREE OR OTHER AND WOULD BE BETTER OFF PLANNING OUR COURSE OF ACTION BASED ON WHAT ACTUALLY EXISTS AS OPPOSED TO THE NONSENSE WE CLAIM EXISTS. THAT IS WHY WHEN I HEAR A POLITICIAN SAY THEY ARE NOT A RACIST I TURN THE CHANNEL IMMEDIATELY!

I had the good fortune to speak with Carl Erskine who pitched the most dominant game I ever saw pitched when he struck out 14 New York Yankees (including Mickey Mantle 4 times 1953 World Series) and Carl Erskine was most proud of having been Jackie Robinson's teammate when Jackie broke the color barrier. That is "good faith" no matter how you were born or raised!

NEW ENGLAND'S RACISM (1943-1968)

I was 4 years old. I either liked someone or I didn't. 4 year old's don't know Black from White. I lived on 25 Houston St. in Waterbury, Connecticut. My next door neighbor was a single guy with a moustache that looked like Willie Sutton, the great American Bank Robber. My mother had a maid. Her skin color was Black. She liked me and I liked her. I used to help her wax wooden floors.

Carl Mancini was mischievious and did his best to see that I was always into some kind of trouble with my parents. He called me over his house and kept talking about the maid's skin color being Black. He instructed me to keep calling her Black on her next day working, over and over. I did so having no idea that I was not just being playful with her. She got into an argument with my mother saying, "Your son had to get that from you! He doesn't know any better!" Then she quit! I remember Carl Mancini laughing his ass off when I told him about it after his perseverent requests that I fill him in on the details.

I was a little kid who did not think at all in terms of Black or White. There were only two Black kids in Mary Abbott Grammar School. Warren Henderson was two years older than me and his sister was one year older than me. I TREATED THEM LIKE I TREATED ALL THE OTHER STUDENTS, WITH HUMAN DECENCY! THEY WERE NOT PEOPLE I KNEW WELL, BUT THEY STRUCK ME AS GOOD KIDS WHO ALWAYS HAD A KIND WORD IN PASSING! IT WAS YEARS LATER I FOUND OUT HOW MUCH WARREN LIKED ME AND ACTUALLY PLAYED A SIGNIFICANT ROLE IN SAVING MY LIFE.

I hadn't thought much about how I treated Warren and his sister because I treated him like I treated everyone else. WHAT I ONLY

FOUND OUT YEARS LATER WAS THAT TREATING WARREN AND HIS SISTER LIKE I TREATED EVERYONE ELSE WAS DIFFERENT THAN EVERYONE ELSE TREATED THEM! THEY WERE THE ONLY BLACK KIDS IN THE GRAMMAR SCHOOL! THEY WERE ALWAYS GOOD TO ME AND ALWAYS HAD A FRIENDLY WORD IN PASSING!

Jackie Robinson

Jackie Robinson broke the color barrier but I was 4 years old in 1947 and by the time I started playing baseball it never occurred to me there was only one Black kid on our team. His name was Vern McKinney and he was built like Mr. Clean and hit the ball out of the park on several occasions. Furthur, he was a great kid and everybody liked him, so again I had no reason to think about Black vs. White.

FULTON PARK BASKETBALL COURT PLAYGROUND

The Black kids came up from the North end. I lived off of Hill Street which was predominantly Italian, Jewish and Irish. THE FEELING WAS THE BLACK KIDS AND THE WHITE KIDS WERE NOT SUPPOSED TO LIKE EACH OTHER. HOWEVER, THE BOTTOM LINE WAS WE NEEDED THEM TO HAVE ENOUGH KIDS TO PLAY BASKETBALL. SO WE GOT ALONG OK, played basketball and had fun. THEN, AFTER THE GAME WE THREW ROCKS AT EACH OTHER SO WE COULD AT LEAST APPEAR NOT TO LIKE EACH OTHER. NOBODY EVER HIT ANYBODY ELSE WE THREW ROCKS FROM SO FAR AWAY AND THEN WE ALL IGNORED IT AND PLAYED FRIENDLY GAMES THE NEXT DAY AND THEN THREW ROCKS FROM VERY FAR AWAY AFTER THE GAME!

THEN THERE WAS BULL HERBERT

Bull Herbert was a senior who occasionally played at Fulton Park when I was a freshman. He was as big as a professional football player and Bull used to like to drive down the middle of the court and knock all the White kids on their ass. While I was complaining about it, my White friend George O'Meara was laughing at me and said, "That's why they call him Bull!"

THE FIRST TIME I REALIZED THE NORTHEAST WAS RACIST!!!

There was a black kid named Carl Spencer who busted his ass and became an excellent basketball player - All-City and 6th man for Providence College when Joe Mullaney was coach. One summer day I had my cousin come down from Torrington, Fred Bredice, All-State in Connecticut, who could shoot as good as Bill Sharman (also went to Cousy's camp -Bob Cousy of the Boston Celtics), Billy Finn who was the greatest basketball player I ever saw in my lifetime, et. al. My mother told me to invite all the kids up for coca-colas and sandwiches after the game -AND THERE WE WENT, ALL THE WHITE KIDS AND CARL SPENCER, WHO WAS BETTER THAN MOST OF THEM AND A GREAT KID! I COULD NOT HELP BUT NOTICE A KIND OF DISPLEASURE AMONG THE NEIGHBORS THAT I NEVER SAW BEFORE! I FIGURED IT OUT A TIME LATER, THAT THEY DID NOT WANT THAT BLACK KID SPENCER IN THE NEIGHBORHOOD! EVEN MORE SHOCKING WAS THAT MY MOTHER WAS ALSO A RACIST IN DENIAL!!!

In 1956 a college kid took me to see Yale play Army at The Yale Bowl in New Haven, Connecticut. It was a big deal because it was the last game the great Army coach Red Blaik ever coached.

He told me about college life at The Citadel, a military academy in South Carolina. I remember his exact words, told in a matter of fact way, "IF THE STUDENTS WERE BORED ON A SATURDAY AFTERNOON WE ALL GOT INTO A CONVERTIBLE, AND THESE OLD NIGGERS WOULD BE SITTING ON A CEMENT PORCH IN A LITTLE SHACK HOUSE AND WE WOULD TRY TO HIT THEM!" I said, "Did you ever hit any body?" He said, "Yes." I said, "What happened?" He said, NOTHING!" I HAD SHOCK AND DISBELIEF AND FELT HE HAD JUST LAYED OUT THE DIFFERENCE BETWEEN THE NORTH AND THE SOUTH IN TERMS OF LEVEL OF DISCRIMINATION!

BOBBY DIGGS

Bobby Diggs was a Black kid that I never recall meeting! Nevertheless, he wanted to shoot and kill me and he had a gun! One freezing winter day I walked down to Dave's Pharmacy on Cooke street, right across the street from Fulton Park, and I ran into Warren Henderson who I hadn't seen in about four years. I had on two bulky sweaters under a red mounted police coat and Warren asked me how I got so big. I told him I had been lifting weights for four years, benched 240 pounds and did quarter squats with 500 pounds and did a clean and jerk with 200 pounds over my head. Warren told Bobby Diggs that I was the biggest baddest mother fucker he had run into in a long time and Bobby Diggs put the word out that he wanted no part of "THAT BERGANTINO!" WARREN HENDERSON SAVED MY LIFE! WHAT GOES AROUND COMES AROUND! BOBBY DIGGS FINALLY DID GET SHOT TO DEATH A FEW YEARS LATER! I DID NOT MOURN HIS DEATH!

AS A JOCK I ALWAYS FOUND THAT WHITE PEOPLE LIKED TO HANG OUT MORE WITH WHITE PEOPLE AND BLACK PEOPLE FELT MORE COMFORTABLE HANGING OUT WITH BLACK PEOPLE! SOO WHILE IT WAS ESSENTIAL THEY WIN THE EQUALITY THAT AT LEAST LEGALLY INSURED SOME IMPROVEMENTS IN HUMAN DECENCY, NEITHER RACE WANTED TO HANG OUT WITH THE OTHER! THIS LOOKS LIKE A TOTALLY RACIST STATEMENT, BUT LOOK AROUND YOU AND SEE IF YOU THINK THE NUMBERS SUPPORT MY CONTENTION!

PARK DEPARTMENT SUPERVISOR 1963

I loved coaching baseball and my players were predominantly Black I ran the place a little like Sgt. Bilko ran his motor pool (Phil Silvers) on the tv show Sgt. Bildo. We played baseball all morning and cards under the bleachers in the hot, sweaty, humity filled afternoons. I remember my boss, Gilmartin, whom I thought was an ungrateful bastard coming by and saying "Hey, Bergantino! You still got morning, noon and night at City Mills Lane?" We won every game until the championship when we got beat by a bunch of 18 year olds in a 12 year old league who lost their birth certificates on a riverboat in Mississippi!

JUNGLE JIM LUSCATOFF

When they asked Abdul Kareem Jabbar why he was so slow getting back down court he said, "HOW WOULD YOU LIKE TO CARRY JUNGLE JIM LUSCATOFF ON YOUR BACK UP AND DOWN

COURT FOR FOUR QUARTERS?" JUNGLE JIM WAS THE HATCHET MAN FOR THE WORLD CHAMPION BOSTON CELTICS, AND NO MATTER OF OTHER TALENTS THOSE WHO LIFTED WEIGHTS AND PLAYED BASKETBALL ASPIRED TO BE ABLE TO DO SOME OF THE THINGS DONE BY JUNGLE JIM LUSCATOFF!

I played basketball on a high school team that drew from 1200 students. There was a high school team named Hartford Buckley that drew from around 3300 students and were in a different class. THEY WERE PREDOMINANTLY BLACK AND IT IS TRUE, AS PORTRAYED IN WODDY HARRELSON'S MOVIE "WHITE GUYS CAN'T JUMP!"

They had a player that had 35 points before half time and we had no chance of stopping him, so the coach says to me: TAKE HIM OUT! SO I DIVED WITH A FLYING LEAP AT AROUND THE FOUL LINE, HIT HIM RIGHT IN THE MIDDLE OF HIS BACK FROM BEHIND, AND HE WENT DOWN SKIDDING ON HIS NOSE INTO THE WOODEN BLEACHERS JUST BEHIND THE BASKET! HE SAID, "MAN, THERE IS GOING TO BE TROUBLE!" I SAID, "WHAT THE FUCK DO YOU THINK THEY SENT ME IN FOR!" HE WAS BLACK AND I WAS WHITE, BUT THAT WAS NOT WHY I HIT HIM FROM BEHIND. THE COACH TOLD ME TO TAKE HIM OUT SO I DID! WHEN OUR BUS LEFT TO GO HOME THERE WERE A COUPLE OF HUNDRED BLACK KIDS PELTING OUR TEAM BUS WITH ROCKS, CALLING US THE DIRTY BASTARDS THAT WE WERE! NO ONE ON THE BUS SAID A WORD ABOUT IT WHICH I THOUGHT WAS STRANGE?

THE FOUR BEST TEAMS IN CONNECTICUT WERE HARTFORD WEAVER AND BUCKLEY AND FROM NEW HAVEN HILLHOUSE AND WILBUR CROSS WHO HAD A BLACK ALL AMERICAN HIGH SCHOOL PLAYER NAMED DAVE HICKS. HILLCREST HAD FOUR BLACK GIANTS AND A LITTLE WHITE GUY AT GUARD WHO HAD THE LAST NAME OF "WHITE".

In my junior year at The University of Connecticut where I majored in political science and minored in history I met football tackle Harry Herbst and the first Black quarterback I ever met, John Billingslea. Harry was German-American. He often said "Billingslea's trouble is he thinks he is White!" They were roommates and appeared to be friends.

In 1964 I just didn't see many Black kids at UCONN. In fact Billingslea was the only one I saw and knew and he was the starting quarterback! AGAIN, AT THAT TIME IN MY LIFE, PRE THERAPY, I WAS AN OBLIVIOUS BASTARD THAT DID NOT NOTICE OR THINK ABOUT VERY MUCH EXCEPT WHAT I HAD FOR HOMEWORK THE NEXT DAY TO PASS MY CLASSES!

THE WATTS RIOTS – 1965

A year after the Watts Riots New Haven, Connecticut had an ALL BLACK COMEDY CLUB THAT WAS THE RAVE OF CONNECTICUT. IT TOOK US A COUPLE OF MONTHS TO GET RESERVATIONS TO SEE AN UP AND COMING COMEDIAN WHO WAS NOT YET WELL KNOWN NATIONALLY NAMED GEOFFREY CHAMBERS. I had a date with Diane Piscatelli and I fixed my good friend George O'Meara up with Diane's first cousin, Judge Piscatelli's daughter. O'Meara was astute but also shitfaced! He had his head on the table with his eyes peering out into the crowd of all black faces when Geoffrey Cambridge walked over to our table and said, "I like your faces! When we take over I am going to let you go!" O'Meara blurts out, "How about just GETTING OUR FUCKING ASSES OUT OF HERE TONIGHT?!?!?" THE ENTIRE BLACK AUDIENCE WAS LAUGHING HYSTERICALLY AND NOTHING HAPPENED TO US AS WE WALKED OUT!

Then I got a flat tire in the heart of Dixwell Avenue, an All-black section of New Haven, Connecticut. I was shitfaced and not astute to the fact we were surrounded by 30 blacks who looked like they wanted to follow up on Watts with us; so O'Meara begins a fake argument that I did not realize was fake. He shouts as loud as he could, "You are not taking me parking with her! Take me back to Waterbury (22 miles) and then come back and go parking. This argument went on for 15 minutes and these 30 Black Would be Rioters were laughing hysterically! They thought we were funnier than Geoffrey Cambridge! We drove off without incident thanks to O'Meara's quick wit! Later on O'Meara got a job as a bullshit artist for a governor of Connecticut, when the Governor had no answer!

The Governor would give George the nod indicating "George, You are On!"

BLACK BASEBALL AND BASKETBALL PLAYERS LOVED ME AS A COACH NOT BECAUSE OF WHAT I KNEW BUT BECAUSE OF WHO I WAS! I WAS UNDEFEATED AS A COACH! I REMEMBER WHEN THE VARSITY BASKETBALL COACH HAD ME COACH A TOURNAMENT GAME IN WHICH HE WAS OUT SICK, ONE OF OUR ALL-STATE BASKETBALL PLAYERS SAID, "YOU DON'T KNOW WHAT THE FUCK YOU ARE DOING, DO YOU!" I RETORTED, "JUST GET THE FUCK OUT THERE AND WIN!" I figured these guys played basketball eight hours a day! x's and O's only counted for so much!

I suppose as a human being from the northeast I felt the Blacks got a raw deal in they didn't have an opportunity to go all the way! The United States clearly was and is a fucked up place on these accounts! Not just for Blacks. As an independent thinker I am supposed to be protected by the first amendment of The United States Constitution but the United States Government has throughout my lifetime done all that they could to insure I wouldn't say or do anything that was out of bounds or violate other control words like being Nice, or Appropriate. And of course I personally identified more with being a mother-fucker who liked to shove my arm up peoples' asses who needed it without any vaseline and built up my personal skill set so I succeeded most of the time! ***THIS CAME ABOUT AS CLOSE TO EXPERIENTIALLY UNDERSTANDING BLACK RAGE AS MY DARK SKINNED COMPATRIOTS WOULD FIND IN "WHITE BOY!"

FOR THIS REASON SOME BLACKS WOULD GIVE ME A BREAK WHERE WHITE FOLKS WOULD NOT! My first job after receiving my doctorate at The University of Southern California was as a Counseling Psychologist then Clinical/Counseling Psychologist GS-12. I thought Veterans were being fucked over all day long every day by The VA Higher Ups and it didn't make any difference if they were Black, Yellow, brown or White!

So in 1973 when Black psychiatrist Paul Logan, M.D. interviewed me to work at the Kedren community Mental Health center in South Central Los Angeles he said "So If you are as good as you say you are why aren't you still working for the VA?" (Metaphorically speaking in an era before terrorists), I said, "I WANTED TO BLOW UP THE VA!" Logan, on the spot said, "You're hired!" I said, "How come? Most people I say that to run the other way!" Logan said, "YOU UNDERSTAND BLACK RAGE!"

I loved the year I worked there and I loved the people I worked with I remember when I started a private practice in Beverly Hills, my father-in-law Herbert Tyson, was kind enough to let me see patients in his condominium in the back room. There was a patient who was about 150 pounds overweight who took buses, 6 hours round trip from South Central Los Angeles to Beverly Hills. She felt that the personal quality I had coaching basketball and baseball made me a one of a kind and it was worth the trip. When I wound down my San Diego private practice a White woman drove up about once a month for three hour sessions. At the heart level Black or White doesn't make any difference. It's human that counts!

THE WHITE MAN'S BURDEN AND THE GRADUAL BUILDING OF RESENTMENT

I received my doctorate in 1971 from The University of Southern California. It was implied that upon receiving my doctorate The world Was my Oyster! This was not the case!. ON EVERY JOB APPLICATION THEY ASKED ME IF I WAS AFRICAN AMERICAN, LATINO, OR A FEMALE! I got so many rejections I was nearly punchdrunk! They didn't care how good I was or that I had a 3.86 GPA!

The only job interviews where they actually cared what I could do was at Georgia State University in Atlanta, where I was interviewed for one hour each by all 12 university counselors. The Chief told me they said, 'I was the best they had ever seen!" Then I asked him how someone like me would do in Atlanta with the Yankee accent? He said, "I'll have you know that Atlanta is the most progressive city in the south. We get people from Minnesota, from Chicago, from New York! Just don't go twelve miles north to Marietta, or they will lynch your Yankee ass in a heartbeat!" I STAYED IN LOS ANGELES!

THE DAY I BECAME AN UNSUNG HERO!

I had a full time job as a junior high school counselor at Hosler Junior High School in Lilly-White Lynwood, California while I was a full time doctoral student at The University of Southern California. Around September, 1970 the first African AMerican kid enrolled. I only met him once! He seemed like a nice enough kid who was a good student who stayed out of trouble! ONE DAY I WALKED OUTSIDE AND FIVE STUDENTS WERE KICKING HIM IN IN THE HEAD WITH ENOUGH FORCE TO KILL HIM!!! I BROKE IT UP EXPECTING TO RECEIVE ACHOLADES FROM THE ADMINISTRATION FOR SAVING THE BOY'S LIFE BY PREVENTING A MURDER! THERE WERE NO WORDS SPOKEN ABOUT IT, ONLY A SUBTLE FEELING THAT I HAD INTERFERED WITH SOMETHING THAT EVERYONE WANTED TO CONTINUE!

Later I found out EVERYONE WAS AFRAID IF THIS ONE BLACK BOY MADE IT BLACKS WOULD MOVE INTO LYNWOOD LOCK, STOCK AND BARREL AND PROPERTY VALUES OF THE RESIDENTS OF LILLY WHITE LYNWOOD WOULD SIGNIFICANTLY DEPRECIATE! THIS IS EXACTLY WHAT HAPPENED. "WHITE BOY'S FEARS WERE JUSTIFIED!" THAT WAS ONE OF THE REASONS THEY HELD A MEETING TO DEFINE THE ROLE OF THE SCHOOL COUNSELOR! I TOOK MY SHOE OFF AND STARTED POUNDING THE TABLE YELLING "I AM THE SCHOOL COUNSELOR AND I WILL DEFINE MY OWN ROLE!" I wasn't about to look the other way or let any murder go down on my watch!

I ALWAYS FIGURED I HAD A SOUL AND I DID NOT WANT TO LOSE IT THAT WAY!

BLACKS WOULD RATHER HANG OUT WITH THEIR OWN KIND!!!

With all the legal hullaballoo about Blacks wanting more integration with Whites, my 77 years experience has shown me that while there are a few exceptions, this is TOTAL AND COMPLETE BULLSHIT! THAT IN FACT; BLACKS FEEL MUCH MORE COMFORTABLE HANGING OUT WITH THEIR OWN AND SO DO WHITES! THAT WAY NEITHER BLACKS OR WHITES HAVE TO HAVE THE CONTINUAL PRESSURE OF "SAYING THE RIGHT THING" IN A POLITICALLY CORRECT MANNER! WHAT BLACK'S WANT IS THE EQUAL OPPORTUNITY TO PURSUE THEIR GOD GIVEN GIFTS IN THE SAME WAY THAT WHITES HAVE RIGHTS. THE BIG SECRET THE WHITES HELD BACK

ON WAS THAT THEY DO NOT HAVE A CLEAR PATH AHEAD TO PURSUE THEIR DREAMS. PERHAPS BLACKS HAVE COME CLOSEST TO WHAT THEY WANT IN PROFESSIONAL SPORTS!

WHITE GUYS USED TO PLAY PRO FOOTBALL AND PRO BASKETBALL

The first time I saw the Minneapolis Lakers on television was 1953. I was ten years old. They had a guard named Slater Martin who was five feet six inches tall. They had another guard named Whitey Sooog who wasn't much bigger!

There were a mix of White and Black and a few of the Black players were great-Bill Russell, Elgin Baylor and Oscar Robertson. The Boston Celtics had White players named Bob Cousy, Easy Ed MacCauley, Tommy Heinsohn and Bill Sharman. The St. Louis Hawks had forward Bob Petit - a great shot from the corner and Clyde Lovellete at Center. The Philadelphia Warriors had Wilt Chamberlin who got 100 points in one game before the 3 second violation rule! WHEN "WHITE BOYS" PLAYED IT WAS A MORE SOPHISTICATED GAME! WITH THE GAME NOW COMPOSED OF PREDOMINANTLY BLACK PLAYERS THE GAME IS MUCH MORE DEPENDENT UPON PHYSICAL HEIGHT, WEIGHT AND BRUTE STRENGTH!. GUYS LIKE BULL HERBERT USED TO HAVE FOULS CALLED ON THEM ALL DAY LONG! WHO WOULD HAVE GUESSED THAT BULL HERBERT WAS TWENTY YEARS AHEAD OF HIS TIME!

In the fifties and early sixties there were a few 285 pound tackles around. They were usually Black. Today 285 is probably close to being the minumum weight for a player to play professional football as a lineman.

While as a youth I played sports seasonally among football, basketball and baseball the only one a "White Boy" can play today without winding up in the hospital is baseball! There is the most balanced of racial mixes among Whites, Blacks and Browns in professional baseball, and their physical sizes are still in the range of human proportions.

BLACKS WILL NOT ROLL OVER ON OTHER BLACKS TO TREAT "WHITE BOY" FAIRLY OR TO SAVE THE BEST AND BRIGHTEST OF THEIR OWN!

I had a much better experience working in an All-Black community mental health center in South Central Los Angeles about eight years after the Watts Riots.

I was always attracted to greatness. It didn't make any difference if skin color was Black, White, brown or Yellow! I was a high school counselor. One Black girl was headed for Harvard, until a Black chemistry teacher gave he a low grade for talking back to him in an argument in which he was clearly wrong! Both the principal and the Superintendent backed the teacher, which would have cost this genius female Black student her chance at Harvard!

I taught her how to file a lawsuit against the Superintendent, the teacher and the Inglewood Unified school District.

The superintendent transferred me out of the counseling office and put me as the counselor of a rubber room where all the kids who got thrown out of school between grades four and twelve were required to write out the same sentence over and over all day long for months at a time and where I was not permitted to speak to any student.

I got bored a lot as a high school counselor. One day I knocked on the classroom door of the high school basketball coach and told him I wanted to coach "the shooters". It was well known in the mid nineties that Black kids couldn't shoot and White kids couldn't jump! He looked like he didn't know what I was talking about, so I yelled, "I CAN'T JUMP!" He said, "Be down the gym at noon hour!

At 56 years old I could whip the living shit out of All-State High School basketball players. The last time I ever played before I ripped a tendon on the bottom of my foot that took three years to heal, I made 83 shots out of 100 from beyond the foul line as far out as the circle!

ON ANOTHER HOT BORING SUMMER DAY I TOOK OFF AND WENT TO a Black woman's class who was the girl's basketball coach. I told her I wanted to counsel a young man who had been held back from graduating by a Mr. Sullivan, an English teacher.

I told him all I wanted to talk about was shooting! Even though he was a Black kid All-State basketball player when he talked about shooting he always referenced two White shooters, Larry Bird and Bill Sharman, in deference to my being White.

The result of my detour was that the woman's basketball coach asked me if I could coach the girl's basketball team in shooting; as she told me the young man I took out of her class told her "Bergantino knew more about shooting than anyone in the world!"

The reason he was held back is because he cut English class first period most mornings. There was a meeting in the counseling office with his mother, Mr. Sullivan, the boy and me. He had his own apartment and his girlfriend used to stay overnight.

He said, "My Sullivan, I really try to come to your English class, but every time I try to get out of bed, my girlfriend starts sucking my cock; I have this big hard on, and I can't bring myself to take my cock out of her I said, "I can't think of anything that would be strong enough motivation to leave that situation for English class! I could remember my days in high school! This guy had every male student's dream! Mr. Sullivan took it personally!

It was summer vacation. The Vice-Principal stated all the counselors were required to attend to program the students who did not attend school for one reason or another during the school year to establish their interests, aptitudes and desires regarding ocurse selection and placement for the following year.

The last month of the regular school year all school counselors were told to place students just to fill up the classes so teachers would know they still had a job. I SAID "THEY WILL ALL BE IN THE WRONG CLASSES!" THE VICE PRINCIPAL SAID NOT TO WORRY ABOUT IT, THEY WOULD BE REASSIGNED WHEN THEY EVENTUALLY SHOWED UP! I WAS THE ONLY WHITE COUNSELOR IN AN ALL BLACK HIGH SCHOOL AND I DID ALL THE WORK WHILE THE TWO BLACK COUNSELORS REFUSED TO PROGRAM ANYBODY.

So there we are programming on my summer vacation without pay and there is a mesomorphic Black soman who continued to stand right behind me close enough that her big Black teats were swinging around my head, at which point, as she was annoying me and was never introduced, I said, "AND SO, WHOM THE FUCK MIGHT YOU BE!" SHE SAID, "I MIGHT BE THE ASSISTANT SUPERINTENDENT OF SCHOOLS AND YOUR ASS ISN'T GOING TO BE HERE ON MONDAY!"

No one would back me in that she claimed I made many mistakes in programming because I was ordered to do so, so and no one told me who she was or that she was there gunning for me!

I got a shitty evaluation that in no way reflected me work or that I was far superior in every way to the two Black counselors. The principal said, "What are you complaining about? You kept your job!" SHE SAID IT IN A WAY THAT MADE IT CLEAR THAT WHITE FOLK WOULD BE GIVEN AN OPPORTUNITY BY BLACK ADMINISTRATORS, BUT NEVER GET AN EVEN BREAK, AND THAT INDEED BLACK IS BEAUTIFUL AND THEREFORE IN THAT SYSTEM THEY ARE AT THE FRONT OF THE LINE NO MATTER WHAT "WHITE BOY" DOES! THEY JUST CAN'T BRING THEMSELVES TO ROLL OVER ON THOSE DESCENDENTS OF FELLOW SLAVE GENERATIONS, AND THEREFORE BLACK ADMINISTRATORS ARE INCAPABLE OF GIVING "WHITE BOY" A FAIR SHAKE NO MATTER WHAT THE FACTS MIGHT BE!

Now of course, after 200 years of slavery this might seem like a small price for 'white boy' to pay, BUT THE WAY I SAW IT AFTER FIFTY YEARS OF CARRYING THE BLACK MAN'S WATER BUCKET, WAS "THEY WEREN"T MY SLAVES AND I AM SICK OF THIS SHIT!"

I AM ALL FOR BLACK, BROWN AND YELLOW FOLK DOING ALL THEY CAN TO GO AS FAR AS THEY CAN IN BETTERING THEMSELVES AND ACTUALLY ATTAINING THE CIVIL RIGHTS IN ACTION THAT THEY HAVE WON! I JUST THINK WE ARE AT THE STAGE OF THE GAME WHERE WHITE BOY HAS TO DO THE SAME THING! WITHOUT THIS YOU HAVE UNDERLYING RESENTMENT GROWING AT THE UNCONSCIOUS LEVEL AND WHITE COPS GUNNING DOWN TWELVE YEAR OLD BLACK KIDS WHO ARE UNARMED!

WHITE BOY IS SICK AND TIRED OF THE FALSE SENSE OF GUILT BLACKS KEEP THROWING AT "WHITE BOY". BLACKS IN THEIR EVERY THOUGHT ARE NOW RIDDEN WITH DEMANDS OF ENTITLEMENT AND THE HOLDING OF "WHITE BOY" ACCOUNTABLE FOR TWO HUNDRED YEARS OF SLAVERY AS IF THE MODERN GENERATION ARE RESPONSIBLE FOR THE ACTIONS OF THEIR ANCESTORS!

AND THEN THEY EXPECT NOT TO GET SHOT IN THE BACK BY "WHITE BOY"! FAT CHANCE OF THAT!

BLACK PRINCIPALS COUNT ON BEING SUPPORTED BY EVIL BLACK SUPERINTENDENTS AND OTHER HIGH RANKING PERSONNEL EVEN WHEN THEY ARE DOING IN THEIR OWN BLACK YOUTH AND BLAMING IT ON WHITE BOY! WHEN THIS OCCURRED ON MY WATCH I SHOVER MY ARM UP THEIR ASSES WITHOUT VASELINE ON EACH AND EVERY OCCASION! I LOVED THE BLACK CHILDREN AS IF THEY WERE MY OWN! I THOUGHT FOR THE MOST PART THE BLACK ADMINISTRATORS WOULD DO BETTER RUNNING CONCENTRATION CAMPS!

One of the jobs I had was with the Los Angeles Unified School District as an elementary school counselor. One Black female counselor and one Black soman Assistant Principal used TO SCREAM AT THE Black kids with shreiks that were deafening and that was their view of counseling.

So one tall lanky sixth grade Black boy, emotionally out of control, comes running into my office as if he is on skate board. The Black kids loved me. This kid happened to be No. 1 on the black counselor and Vp blood curdling scream list. HE SHOWED ME HIS HANDS AND THEY WERE ALL WHITE AND THE SKIN WAS PEELED OFF OF THEM! I SAID, "WHAT HAPPENED TO YOUR HANDS?" HE SAID, "IT IS NO GOOD TO BE BLACK SO I PEELED ALL THE SKIN OFF MY HANDS UNTIL THEY WERE WHITE!" I FELT SO BAD FOR HIM I ALMOST CRIED!

SO I WROTE A PAPER CALLED "THE BLACK BITCH SYNDROME" AND SENT IT TO ALL THE COUNSELORS IN THE LOS ANGELES UNIFIED SCHOOL DISTRICT. THE THEME WAS THAT THE BLOOD CURDLING SCREAMS OF THE BLACK BITCHES LEFT THE BLACK YOUTH OF AMERICA WITH SUCH LOW SELF ESTEEM THEY WANTED TO SKIN THEMSELVES TO BE WHITE!

At the time I wrote this article I already had 100 publications that went to professional audiences in the field of humanistic psychology, psychotherapy and music. It struck me as strange this was the only article I wrote that a general public magazine expressed interest in publishing -"PSYCHOLOGY TODAY". As I did not want an illustrious professional legacy to be defined by THE BLACK BITCH SYNDROME I CHOSE NOT TO HAVE THE ARTICLE PUBLISHED!

The principal, Al Edwards, insisted I stand outside knowing that people in the community who misunderstood what I stated would merely dismiss me as a White Racist, and more than likely shoot me with a gun! When I confronted Al Edwards with his attempted murder scheme he did not deny it, but merely said, "Unless you want to be fired immediately you will stand outside in public view when school is dismissed every day!"

Al felt he could get away with murder because his fraternity brother at an all Black college from Louisiana was Assistant Supt. of Schools.

Al refused to give one White teacher any books for his students and then threatened to fire him because his students did not do as well as black teachers on statewide examinations!

DISCLAIMER IF YOU ARE AN AMERICAN, YOU ARE A RACIST AND TO DENY IT IS TOTAL AND COMPLETE BULLSHIT! THE WAY TO GO IS TO LEARN YOUR OWN COUNTERTRANSFERENCE WHICH IS WHAT THIS BOOK IS ATTEMPTING TO SHOW YOU SOME OF THE THINGS TO LOOK FOR IN YOURSELF AND THEN SEE HOW IT PLAYS OUT RACIALLY!

MY AMERICAN INTRODUCTION TO FIDEL CASTRO IS A COMMIE BASTARD WHO JOINED WITH THE RUSSIANS TO HAVE MISSLES BROUGHT TO CUBA AND IF IT WERE NOT FOR THE GOOD GRACES OF BOTH NIKITA KRUSCHEV AND PRESIDENT JOHN FITZGERALD KENNEDY WOULD HAVE GOTTEN THE WORLD AS WE KNOW IT BLOWN TO KINGDOM COME IN A NUCLEAR WAR!. BAD MAN, RIGHT?!?!?!?! (1963)

SOMEWHERE AROUND 2012 I SAW AN OLD FILM CLIP OF FIDEL CASTRO BEING INTERVIEWED IN MIAMI BEACH WHEN BATTISTA WAS STILL IN POWER IN CUBA. CASTRO SAID, "I LOVE THE UNITED STATES! I LOVE BASEBALL! I WAS A FIRST BASEMAN! I TRIED OUT FOR THE ST. LOUIS CARDINALS AND DID NOT MAKE IT! I LOVE AMERICA!"

WHEN I HEARD THIS I FELT DUPED BY GOVERNMENT PROPAGANDA AND I WONDERED WHAT THE HELL THE

UNITED STATES GOVERNMENT DID TO CASTRO AND CUBA TO TURN HIM FROM THAT STATEMENT TO THE LEADER OF THE CUBAN REVOLUTION AND HATED DICTATOR?

As a psychoanalyst I learned to empty my mind of all preconceptions and make my mind a blank slate without prejudging anything. I found this to be the only way a person could come closer to the truth if they wanted to. From kindergarten through my first doctorate at The University of Southern California took 22 years. After getting my doctorate at USC I treated myself to a vacation in Scandinavia.

THERE ARE ONLY BLACK AND WHITE INDIVIDUALS – DO NOT TREAT INDIVIDUALS AS RACES

I was on a boat from Malmo, Denmark to Lund University in Sweden. I had a doctorate from USC! The boat Captain said, "You are not as dumb as most Americans!" It took me 22 years of education in American Schools. I felt ripped off by American Education and began reading British books! They were more honest in perspective!

I got shipped out of Al Edward's Black shark tank to Griffith Park as a counselor to deal with racism. There was a Black fat woman peer counselor put in charge of keeping me muzzled in that they didn't particularly care who lived or died in this racial group of mostly Black kids, 20% Hispanic, one English and one German kid. The White Boys looked like they just got out of Buchenwald! Gaunt! They were not thriving and were terrified to say a word. They paid me to sit and watch the O.J. Simpson trial and later sit in a barracks and study Italian with my own tapes before they imposed an agreement upon me in which my services to Los Angeles Unified would cease BECAUSE WHAT I SAID WAS NOT POLITICALLY CORRECT! LAUSD HAD A POLICY IN OPERATION THAT WAS TANTAMOUNT TO "FUCK THE FIRST AMENDMENT!"

THE DISTRICT HAD AN ITALIAN GUY ROOTING FOR ME WHO WAS NOT ALLOWED TO ROOT FOR ME BECAUSE HE REPRESENTED THE DISTRICT!. I HAD A LAWYER! I SAID, "WHY DON'T YOU GUYS GO OUTSIDE AND GIVE ME TWENTY MINUTES WITH THAT BLACK BASTARD!" I KEPT SHOUTING IT OVER AND OVER! THE ITALIAN GUY WAS LAUGHING HIS

ASS OFF! AL EDWARDS KEPT YELLING "I DON'T HAVE TO TAKE THIS SHIT!" I KEPT YELLING TO AL EDWARDS, "YES YOU DO!!!" THE POLITICS WERE THAT HE COULD GET RID OF ME ONLY BECAUSE HIS BLACK BROTHERS WOULDN'T ROLL OVER ON ANOTHER SLAVE, RIGHT, WRONG OR INDIFFERENT!: BUT I COULD DO ANYTHING BUT PUNCH THE SHIT OUT OF HIM ON THE WAY OUT!!! WHICH I DID!!!

NOW WHAT DID "BLACK BOY" DO TO WHITE BOY THAT TURNED A HARMLESS AMERICAN RACIST FROM THE NORTHEAST INTO A COUNTER TRANSFERRENTIALLY FREE "WHITE BOY" ALREADY TERMED A REVERSE OREO BY A BLACK WOMAN AT KEDREN COMMUNITY MENTAL HEALTH CENTER IN SOUTHCENTRAL LOS ANGELES INTO A GUY FED UP TO HIS EYEBALLS WHO NOW HAD A NEED TO SUPPORT BLACKS WHILE NOT CUTTING HIS OWN BALLS OFF (THE BLACK REQUEST THAT IS AT THE BOTTOM OF LITTLE BLACK KIDS GETTING SHOT IN THE BACK BY WHITE COPS!) YELLING, "LET ME AT THAT BLACK BASTARD FOR TWENTY MINUTES!" I SUSPECT THIS IS HOW THE UNITED STATES TURNED CASTRO FROM A FIRST BASEMAN WHO LOVED BASEBALL AND AMERICA TO A CRAZED COMMIE! PSYCHOANALYTICALLY IT IS CALLED "SEVERE PATHOLOGICAL PROJECTIVE IDENTIFICATION" OR AS TRANSACTIONAL ANALYSIS CLINICIANS WROTE "THE PUTTING THE HOT POTATO INTO THE OTHER GUY'S GUTS!" THIS LEAVES BOTH THE BLACK MAN AND THE WHITE MAN FEELING THEY MUST DEFEND THEIR OWN PRESERVATION OF SELF, SELF RESPECT AND SELF ESTEEM AT ALL COST! THIS OFTEN GETS TRANSLATED INTO "IF YOU FUCK WITH ME ONE MORE TIME, I AM GOING TO PUT A BULLET UP YOUR BLACK TWELVE YEAR OLD ASS!"

It is easy for a Black kid to get a White cop not to shoot him! ALL HE HAS TO SAY IS "YES SIR!" BUT HE CAN'T SAY IT! I have written ten books. When you read all of them and chew up, digest and integrate the anomaly of words that cut across many fields of Education in the pursuit of "TO BE OR NOT TO BE' YOU WLL HAVE ALL YOU NEED TO TRANSFORM YOUR BODILY FORM INTO A HEAVENLY BODY! UNTIL SUCH TIME I WILL NOT BE REPEATING THE

ORDINARY CONVERSATIONAL ENGLISH THAT I SPEW FORTH BECAUSE IT IS NOT REPEATABLE!

As for the Black kids that would rather get shot in the ass than call THE WHITE COP, SIR, IT IS A SIMPLE BUT CUMULATIVELY ANNOYING MATTER THAT HAS TO DO WITH DISRESPECT AND THE INSULTING AND DESTRUCTION OF SELF ESTEEM ON THE PART OF BOTH WHITE AND BLACK. THE PROBLEM CURRENTLY IS IN A COUNTRY WHERE EVERYONE INFLICTS EITHER HIGH LEVEL OR LOW LEVEL RACIAL DISCRIMINATION ON A DAILY BASIS NO ONE ADMITS TO IT! THEY SAY, "I AM NOT A RACIST!" THIS BOOK DEALS WITH THE COUNTERTRANSFERENCE OF THE WRITER TO DEMONSTRATE HOW THE ACCUMULATION OF LITTLE THINGS OVER THE YEARS GETS TO BE A FUCKING PAIN IN THE ASS! AND IN TODAY'S MODERN WORLD EVEN ACTED OUT IN THE FORM OF MURDER THAT THE MURDERER DOES NOT KNOW THAT HE HAS DONE BECAUSE IT IS ALL BELOW THE SURFACE OR THAT THE VICTIM ACKNOWLEDGES HE OR SHE HAS PLAYED A ROLE IN EVOKING SUCH VIOLENCE! BLACKS ARE THE LOUDEST IN CLAIMING THEY SHOULD RECEIVE A FREE LUNCH ON THIS BECAUSE OF THE TRANSGRESSIONS OF OUR BRETHERN THAT WERE AT THE ROOTS OF A CIVIL WAR! THIS DENIAL AND PROJECTING OF GUILT ONTO WHITE BOY IS ONE SURE WAY TO GET A BULLET RIGHT IN THE ASS!

ENCOUNTERS WITH DIZZY
GILLESPIE AND MILES DAVIS

Before my first book came out and I developed an international reputation training psychotherapists around the world (Psychotherapy Insight & Style: The Existential Moment -288 pp. Allyn & Bacon, Inc. Boston, 1981) I wrote Dizzy Gillespie a letter proposing he and I do a workshop together for musicians whereby I would work with their heads and he would work with them musically. My father was a professional musician and I knew most of the the Musician's Union Local 186 members since I was six years old. Diz used to come to a club on LaBrea and Washington run by saxaphone player and friend of Diz Red Holloway. I didn't hear anything for 3 months and was not expecting a response. One Saturday afternoon about 3 p.m. I get a call from someone who was high and said, "Let's Make Some Money and Let's Have Some Fun!" I said, 'Whose this!" He said, "This is The Diz! That's what you wrote to me, isn't it?" I said, "I will come down to see you at night!" I got two other shrinks and my wife at the time and the DIZ was funny, high on marijuana. I went up to him during the break to pursue what I wrote to him about in terms of doing a workshop together. DIZ SAID, "WHY DON'T YOU GET YOUR OWN THING! THAT WAY YOU WON"t HAVE TO SUCK SHIT OUT OF A NIGGER'S ASS!" I LEFT IMMEDIATELY AND NEVER LISTENED TO ANY OF HIS MUSIC AGAIN, AND FRANKLY DID NOT LIKE HIM AT ALL AFTER THAT EPISODE!

<u>MILES DAVIS AND ME AT BURT BACHARACH'S CHRISTMAS PARTY IN 1987</u>

I heard that Miles hated White people and they fucked him over enough that he had a solid justification to hate them! Burt sat Miles and I at the same dinner table. Burt told him I was a trumpet player. Miles said, "Whose your favorite trumpet player? I said, "Chet Baker, but you are second!" Miles and I had an instant heart to heart affection for each other. I told him I hadn't played trumpet since my doctoral work at USC but was playing mandolin and had studied a few years with Mischa shenkyman, The Paganini of the Mandolin from the Soviet Union. We had a blast together! When Miles left he wanted to acknowledge me and that he had a good time hanging out with me, so he said in that gruffled voice of his, in front of the entire crowd, "You gotta practice Man! You gotta practice!" I was lit! Three sheets to the wind, so I said, "Hey Miles, Fuck you! You gotta practice! You play trumpet and I play mandolin! You gotta practice!" Everyone there knew that was true and Miles, the entire crowd and myself all broke out in hysterical laughter. I became a professional musician from 1996 to 2012 and it took me five hours practice a day on the trumpet and two hours a day on the mandolin! Trumpet was an absolute mother fucker because I never knew who was going to show up, depending upon the physical wellness of my body. For that reason alone, it was much easier to be consistent on the mandolin. Maynard Ferguson told me that he practiced so much so no one except himself would know how bad he was!

Dr. Art Farmer - played the best one nighter I ever heard on a gold plated flumpet -which was half way in size between a cornet and a trumpet. I wanted to take a jazz trumpet lesson from him when he came to the jazz educator's conference in Long beach around 2003. Art lived in France but I tracked him down and we talked for about a half hour. This guy was a great jazz player, but he was afraid he didn't know any jazz and couldn't teach it. I asked him why he stayed in Paris instead of coming back to the United States. He said, "When I walk down the street in Paris everybody says, 'There's Dr. Art Farmer, the great jazz trumpet player'. When I walk down the street in the United States everybody says, 'there's that Nigger, who plays trumpet, Art Farmer! I am never coming back to stay!" Art had no axe to grind with me and you certainly had to take him seriously regarding his feelings about being on the wrong end of racial prejudice.

I LIKE SOME BLACKS AND OTHERS I DON'T!

LOOK INTO AN AFRICAN AMERICAN'S EYES!!!!

If you see a dead looking non-responsive look as though there is no feeling in his or her body, and there is no response to anything human about you, YOU ARE THE VICTIM OF REVERSE RACISM! IF YOU ARE WHITE YOU WILL GET SCREWD OVER! IT IS JUST A MATTER OF WHERE AND WHEN!

The Vice-Principal at Morningside High School, or at least one of them was a man named Lou Thomas. He was friendly and had no bones to pick and was helpful to me in every way that he could be. Furthur, he was an excellent tenor saxaphone player and when he knew I wanted experience in learning to play jazz he invited me to sit in every Sunday in an All Black Club named LaLousiann with an All Black bandled by a drummer named Lerman. Lerman and I didn't like each other very much but they had a piano player named Bobby Blevins and Lou who were quite helpful to me.

LERMAN AND BLACK WOMENS' PANTIES

At the end of every Sunday Lerman would whip out a huge size of panties pointing out that they could not be the panties of White women but were a size that were much more likely to fit the Black Sisters! The Black

Women always were good natured about these huge panties and they drew the most laughs each and every week no matter how many times Lerman did the same thing!

WHEN UNCLE REMUS WAS AROUND WHITE KIDS WERE NOT AFRAID OF BLACK MEN! THE NAACP. FUCKED THAT ALL UP!!!

When I was a young boy there was a movie called SONG OF THE SOUTH THAT WOULD COME BACK TO THE THEATRES EVERY SO OFTEN. I think it originally came out in the late thirties or early forties.

You had the story of Brer Rabbit, Brer Fox, brer Bear being told to White and Black kids alike by Uncle Remus -a kindly old Black Gentleman that sang Zipidee -do-da; zipidee Ay; Oh, what a wonderful day!" Every White kid I ever met loved Uncle Remus and this feeling carried over to how White people felt about Black people. The NAACP had Disney pull the movie saying it gave both Whites and Blacks the idea that Uncle Remus and black men were Uncle Toms! Uncle Remus got chewed out a few times by a chite woman who owned the plantation but everyone could tell she just looked like a maniac who was mean and Uncle Remus was a great guy!

Song of the South was pulled around the time Malcomb X, Stokely Carmichael, Rapp Brown and Eldridge Clever were into Black people fighting back with violence against civil injustice. There is no way a non-Black White Dude like myself could comment on the Black solutions to the problem. I AM ONLY COMMENTING ON WHAT WHITE BOY PERCEIVED ALONG THE WAY AND A LOT OF WHITES WHO TALKED TO ME ABOUT THESE ISSUES!.

For example, BLACK FOLK WHO WERE GETTING FUCKED OVER, ARRESTED AND BEATEN PHYSICALLY IN THE SYSTEM, WOULD CROSS THE STREET WHERE THERE WAS NO LIGHT AND LEGALLY MAKE WHITE BOY WAIT FOREVER! HAVING BEEN ONE OF THOSE WAITING ON MORE THAN ONE OCCASION I ALWAYS HAD A FEW CHOICE THOUGHTS AND COMMENTS FOR MY COMPANION INSIDE THE AUTOMOBILE.

STEPHEN FETCHET was a movie actor in the early thirties who played this lazy shifless slow walking "Nigger" with a shuffle that later became the Black Man's way of retaliation. THE NAACP WAS QUITE RIGHT TO GET RID OF THIS IMAGE COMPLETELY AS IT BOTH GAVE BLACKS A BAD NAME AND WAS USED BY THEM AS A PASSIVE AGGRESSIVE METHOD OF RETALIATION AGAINST WHITE FOLK WHO WERE NOT THE PERPETRATORS!

IN OTHER WORDS MY ENTIRE LIFETIME WAS SPENT PAYING OFF DEBT FOR THE SINS OF MY FOREFATHERS THROUGH A FALSE SENSE OF GUILT, AND I HAVE HAD IT UP TO MY ASS WITH THIS FALSE SENSE OF GUILT BULLSHIT! TREAT BLACKS FAIRLY! DON'T FUCK THEM OVER! GIVE THEM THEIR CIVIL RIGHTS! DON'T TELL EVERYONE THEY WANT TO HANG OUT WITH WHITE PEOPLE WHEN THEY DO NOT! WHAT THEY WANT ARE THE CIVIL RIGHTS GRANTED TO WHITE PEOPLE WITHOUT GETTING TARGETTED BY POLICE, DENIED CIVIL RIGHTS AND BEING SHOT IN THE BACK! THEY ARE ENTITLED TO ALL THESE THINGS! WHITE JUSTICE SHOULD INCLUDE BLACKS ON EQUAL FOOTING AS FAR AS AMERICAN CIVIL RIGHTS! BLACKS HAVE TO STOP ANTAGONIZING THE WHITE FOLK WHO THEY WANT TO BACK THEIR PLAY! OTHERWISE WE ARE JUST IN FOR ONE HOT BLOODY SUMMER AFTER ANOTHER!.

HOME RUN DERBY -mid 1950's

1.　Mickey Mantle - White from Commerce, Oklahoma
2.　Willie Mays -Black -Negro League and New York Giants
3.　Henry Aaron - Milwaukee braves

This was in the relative beginnings of their careers. White announcer. Racial slurs unintentional and taken for granted. Both Willy Mays and Henry Aaron looked frightened, as if someone might shoot them for being Black guys on the show. This was after Jackie Robinson broke the color line in 1947 and I did not notice these things when I saw Home Run Derby in the 50's but I was shocked in all that I had missed when I saw it rerun in 2019. It is hard to think about playing great baseball when you are in constant fear of getting a bullet up your ass!

When I saw Jackie ROBINSON HE WAS AN EXCELLENT BASEBALL PLAYER, BUT NOT IN THE GREATEST CATEGORIES OF MANTLE, MAYS OR AARON.

THE THING I REMEMBER MOST IS THAT HE DIED AT AROUND 56 or 58 years old with all grey hair looking like a very old man. In retrospect I think he would have lived longer and healthier had he not broken the color barrier in professional baseball, but perhaps then he wouldn't have been Jackie Robinson!

BLACK AND WHITE IN THE SUNNY SOUTH

I do not have direct experience in that I never lived in the South. So what I will write about is the intensity of the primitive countertransfernce of some persons I knew from the South in relation to blacks.

I do recall my first trip to New Orleans. The bus driver said, "We like you Yankees down here! We want you to have a good time and we will do our best to show you a good time AND THEN WE WANT YOU TO GO HOME! WE DO NOT WANT YOU TO STAY!

I was applying to graduate school in 1965 and I applied to The University of Mississippi. I didn't hear anything so I borrowcd $10,000 student loan from the United States Government and paid my tuition at Fairfiel University in Connecticut, I had two roommates and a 6 room house on the beach.

Around September 6th I got a call from the Dean at the University of Mississippi. He said, "I am calling you to tell you that your fellowship has come through and WE WELCOME YOU AT THE UNIVERSITY OF MISSIPPI!" I explained the situation and then said, "I have one more question. Why are you calling me now/ the semester started two weeks ago!" He said, 'Frankly, I AM JUST GETTING AROUND TO IT!" There wasn't an obsessive bone in his body. That was quite different than the hard driving Northeast!

The first job after my doctorate was with the Veterans Administration in West Los Angeles. There was a whiz kid from the South who was the head of social services at 26 years old; who had a psychiatrist referring patients to him in private practice and who was pursuing his doctorate at The University of Southern California. Furthur, he had a knockout looking wife!

The problem was they both liked to go to s club in Marina del Rey and look at the beautiful people several nights a week. I wasn't there but the story he told me was that he got drunk and was creating a loud situation when a big Black police officer told him to be quiet and calm down. THEN HE BEGAN TO TELL THE POLICEMAN, "Listen you nigger! If you did that down south we would lynch you." The policeman kept beating his head with a flashlight which did not deter this fellow from his barrage of racial slurs. His face looked like raw hamburger or a piece of Italian saugage hanging in the window before it is cooked. THE MAN KNEW HIMSELF WELL ENOUGH TO KNOW HE HAD LITTLE CONTROL AT THE DEEPEST PRIMITIVE LEVEL REGARDING THE FEELINGS HE WAS RAISED WITH, SO HE QUITE HIS JOB, THE DOCTORAL PROGRAM AND MOVED BACK DOWN SOUTH! He received his doctorate from a top notch Southern University and became a successful clinical psychologist in private practice. He knew his clinical limitations RACIALLY AND CUT HIS LOSSES WHILE HE STILL COULD! THIS MAN HAD EXTRAORDINARY MENTAL DISCIPLINE TO MAKE SUCH LIFE ALTERING DECISIONS IN TWO WEEKS AND CUT BAIT!

I didn't know much about Alabama and in 1972 I had a private practice patient from Alabama that was as hot a looking Southern Woman as I had ever seen! I asked her if she ever heard of Bear Bryant. SHE SAID, "OH, THE BEAR WALKS ON WATER IN THE SEXIEST WAY I HAD EVER HEARD! IT WAS AFTER THAT COMMENT THAT I STARTED WATCHING ALABAMA FOOTBALL IN ADDITION TO USE FOOTBALL!

THE SOUTHERN GENTLEMAN COULD HAVE SAID "YES SIR! TO THE BLACK POLICE OFFICER AND HIS HEAD WOULD NOT HAVE BEEN BEATEN WITH A LONG FLASHLIGHT UNTIL IT LOOKED LIKE A RAW PIECE OF SAUSAGE HANGING IN THE WINDOW OF AN ITALIAN DELI; JUST AS THE TWELVE YEAR OLD UNARMED BLACK KID COULD HAVE STOPPED RUNNING AWAY FROM THE WHITE POLICE OFFICER AND SAID "YES, SIR!" IN WHICH CASE HE WOULD STILL BE ALIVE TODAY! BUT RACIAL PREJUDICES GO SO DEEP NEITHER THE BLACK BOY NOR THE WHITE MAN COULD BRING THEMSELVES TO ENDURE SUCH REAL OR IMAGINED DEGREES OF SELF RESPECT AND OR SELF ESTEEM SO AS TO SAVE THEIR OWN LIVES!! MAN, THIS IS SERIOUS SHIT FOR WHICH I AM PROPOSING THE FIRST STEP AND THEN SEE

WHAT DEVELOPS FROM THERE! THE FIRST STEP IS "DON'T DENY THAT IF YOU ARE BORN IN AMERICA YOU ARE A FUCKING RACIST AND IT IS JUST A MATTER OF TIME AND PLACE AS TO WHEN IT REARS IT'S UGLY HEAD!!!!!!!!!!!!!!

SOFT EYES

I AM WHITE FROM THE TOP OF MY HEAD TO THE TIP OF MY TOES AND IF SOMEONE OF ANOTHER RACE LOOKS AT ME WITH SOFT AND SOMEONE ALIVE LOOKING EYEBALLS THEY HAVE THEIR RACISM UNDER CONTROL WITHIN NORMAL LIMITS AND ARE NOT DANGEROUS IN TERMS OF PRESENTING ANY CLEAR AND PRESENT DANGER THAT WILL BE IMMEDIATELY ACTED OUT!

I LIKED PLAYING JAZZ MORE WITH BLACKS BECAUSE I WOULD FEEL MORE OF MYSELF IN DOING SO. THEY WERE AS A GROUP NOT AS PROFICIENT AS THE WHITE PLAYERS WHO COULD READ MUSIC BETTER AND EVEN PERFORM BETTER TECHNICALLY, BUT THEY HAD AN ACCESS TO THE PRIMITIVE SELF MOST WHITE JAZZ PLAYERS DO NOT HAVE!

I TOOK A JAZZ CAMP TO LEARN TO PLAY JAZZ IN 1998 in Louisville, Kentucky at the Jamie Abersoll Jazz Camp. Morning activities included going to an academically oriented class where musical concepts and notations were written on the Blackboard I was back in bed ten minutes later. I got assigned to a Black Jazz Educator who played organ and taught at Ohio state University. His name was Hank Marr. In the afternoon I was in a group composed of a tenor saxaphone, piano, drums, bass fiddle, trombone, guitar and me on trumpet. The idea was everybody takes a turn. When it got to me I said, "I don't know how to play jazz." Hank Marr said, "Well, go home then!" He forced my hand and what came out was the kind of jazz I heard on the KJAZZ radio station for 30 years. It was so good other students started calling me "Father Time" and Hank Marr asked me if I wanted to know what I was doing. I said "No", this is jazz and I'm never going to play exactly the same thing again! I thought memorized licks were bullshit! You either could play jazz or you couldn't! This is why Miles loved me and I loved him! Nothing was repeatable!

I began my first private practice in the Hillcrest area of San Diego at the Phoenix Center for Psychology on 3760 Third Avenue It was owned by

Dr. Javad Emami, Ph.D., clinical psychologist who became President of the San Diego Society of clinical Psychologists in 1974. He claimed Americans were racists in that they did not like Iranians! He was way ahead of his time! At the time I thought he was full of bullshit!

I had a private practice primarily composed of Naval Personnel from Coronado. A couple of referrals were assassins for the United States Government. This was a bit shocking to me. One of them wanted to work on his guilt feelings in that he was caught between God and country. He was a Roman Catholic. It was a mortal sin for which you were condemned to hell for all eternity to murder someone yet that is what the United States government had him doing! Not in war, but individual assassinations!

The second Navy Murderer came in, looked me right in the eye and said (in 1973) I HATE NIGGERS! I HATE JAPS! I HATE WOPS! I HATE CHINKS! AND MOST OF ALL I HATE HIPPIES!" I was wearing blue dungaree denims, and shirt and I had a beard. I LOOKED HIM SQUARE IN THE EYE WITH A FURY OF MURDEROUS RAGE SEETHING OUT OF ME TOWARD HIM AND I SAID "WHAT THE FUCK DOES THAT HAVE TO DO WITH ME!!!" Once he knew I, too, was capable of murderous rage the work could begin!

Somewhere in the mid nineties I went to a psychology conference and the black psychologist was stating one politically correct platitude after another about Blacks and Whites, using that reverse discrimination and false sense of guilt. White boy ought to have, so when he asked if anybody had a question I said, "No, but I have a statement to make!" (As questions are merely a way to torture other people) then I told him the San Diego story about the government assassins from the United States Navy and how I handled it. The entire place was in shock and speechless. I got up and walked out. A psychologist who was younger than me but older than them said, "Hey Bergantino, You are a hot shit!"

THE AMERICAN PSYCHOLOGICAL ASSOCIATION WAS ASKING ME TO CUT MY OWN BALLS OFF WITH THIS RACIALLY APPROPRIATE BULLSHIT! I DON'T DO THAT FOR ANYBODY!!! IT WAS AT THAT MOMENT I COMPLETELY LOST INTEREST IN BEING A CLINICAL PSYCHOLOGIST. I RESPECTED ROSA PARKS WHO FOUGHT FOR HER SEAT ON THE FRONT OF THE BUS! I SAW THE AMERICAN PSYCHOLOGICAL AS WELL AS STATE ORGANIZATIONS AND LICENSING BOARDS AS COERCING PSYCHOLOGISTS TO

NOT EXIST AS IN DO NOT BE THERE WHEN YOU TREAT PATIENTS AND INSIST PSYCHOLOGISTS RUN TO THE BACK OF THE BUS FOR A SEAT!

That was the beginning of my war against psychology licensing boards AS THEY ONLY CREATED THE ILLUSION OF SAFETY WHILE KILLING ANY DEVELOPMENT IN PSYCHOLOGISTS THAT MIGHT BE HEALING!

So I retired from the private practice of clinical psychology and I have excerpted a few paragraphs from a WOULD YOU NAME YOUR KID WHITEY FORD?

Mickey Mantle said Whitey Ford was one of the three best pitchers he ever faced in the 1950's! Whitey Lockman used to play first base for the New York Giants baseball team at the Polo Grounds and "Whitey and Barone" had a gas station in the North Square of Waterbury, Connecticut. The North square was to Waterbury as Harlem was to New York! I haven't heard of a White kid being named Whitey since 1970 or after the Watts Riots and politically correct ruled the roost. Not that I would give a shit only it rubs me the wrong way allowing resentment to accumulate with other politically correct bullshit. AGAIN, I WON'T CUT MY OWN DICK OFF FOR ANYBODY AND I MAKE NO FUCKING APOLOGIES FOR IT!

BROWNS OR LATINOS. I DID NOT WRITE ABOUT THEM BECAUSE I DID NOT GROW UP WITH THEM AND I DO NOT KNOW THEM WELL ENOUGH TO HAVE MUCH TO SAY IN THE REALM OF PSYCHOLOGICAL PRIMITIVE EXPERTISE!

RIO DE JANEIRO, BRAZIL IN 2003

I went down there to study Choro Music -the music of the people since around 1850. Furthur, the lead instrument is a bandolim which is a little bigger than a mandolin and cuts a bit more but is not as mellow. When I got there on a Saturday at noon, I bought a bandolim at Gold's Music Store that I had made for me prior to arrival. I sat in a circle with the locals, fine musicians, and played choro. There was one man leaning against a pole in the store the entire time, and when we finished he looked at me and said "NOT BAD FOR A GRINGO" A TERM USED TO INSULT AMERICANS BUT SAID TO ME IN AN AFFECTIONATE ACCEPTING WAY THAT MADE ME FEEL WELCOME! BLACKS

AND WHITES OUGHT TO KEEP THIS STORY IN MIND IN TERMS OF HOW THEY TREAT EACH OTHER, AND ALWAYS COP TO YOUR OWN REVERSE RACIAL DISCRIMINATION IF YOU DON'T WANT A BULLET UP YOUR ASS!

Furthur, are a few excerpts from my direct supervisor when working in an All Black Community as a high school counselor. Out of all that was written I felt these two paragraphs were the most important in terms of going along and getting along as a white man in an All black community! "DR. BERGANTINO HAS TREATED ALL CHILDREN AT MORNINGSIDE HIGH SCHOOL AS IF THEY WERE HIS OWN", BE THEY AFRICAN AMERICAN OR CHICANO HE HAS SEEN TO IT THAT THE UNDERPRIVILEGED HAVE UNDERSTOOD AND LEARNED HOW TO AGGRESSIVELY MOVE IN THE SYSTEM IN WHICH THEY NEED TO BECOME THE KIND OF CITIZENS WHO WILL DO WELL IN LIFE."

"IN TERMS OF ADMINISTRATIVE CAPACITY, SHOULD DR. BERGANTINO WISH TO MOVE TO AN ASSISTANT PRINCIPAL OR PRINCIPAL POSITION, WHAT HE HAS DEMONSTRATED IN MEETINGS IS AN UNUSUAL EXPERIENTIAL CAPACITY OF HOW TO UTILIZE PERSONAL AUTHORITY AS IT RELATES TO THE CHAIN OF COMMAND. HE HAS AN UNCANNY SENSE OF WHERE AUTHORITY AND RESPONSIBILITY MUST BE CONGRUENT THROUGH THE ADMINISTRATIVE HIERARCHY FOR EFFECTIVE EDUCATION TO OCCUR ON A SUSTAINED BASIS. DR. BERGANTINO HAS EXCELLENT LEADERSHIP CAPACITY. I RECOMMEND DR. BERGANTINO WITHOUT RESERVATION." WRITTEN BY THE REVEREND DR. LEN BERGANTINO

See website for other books drbergantino.com

Xlibris

GERMANS – JEWS – HOLOCAUSTS
and
THE COLLECTIVE UNCONSCIOUS

 DR. LEN BERGANTINO, Ed.D., Ph.D.

GERMANS – JEWS – HOLOCAUSTS *and* THE COLLECTIVE UNCONSCIOUS

DR. LEN BERGANTINO, Ed.D., Ph.D.

X

POLITICAL PSYCHOLOGY
INVASIONS

ISBN 978-1-7960-8444-3

9 781796 084443

51999

Xlibris

When Baseball was King
The New York Yankees were
King of Baseball

The Reverend Dr. Len Bergantino is a multi-faceted individual who achieved international prominence in the areas of psychoanalysis, psychotherapy, clinical psychology, and music. His other fields include education and religion, with a precursory knowledge of medicine and law. He is a weathervane in terms of knowing the right thing to do and has the temperament of Che Guevarra in getting it done!

When the Reverend Dr. Len Bergantino grew up, the first thing he had in mind was to wear number 22 and take over for Allie Reynolds, the Super Chief, as the mainstay of the Mound Staff of the NEW YORK YANKEES!!! The New York Yankees won 5-world series in a row. (1949-1953) !!!

Xlibris

ISBN 978-1-7960-7891-6
90000
9 781796 078916

RoseDog🐾Books

The Reverend Dr. Len Bergantino, Ed.D., Ph.D.

From 2012 through 2018, Len Bergantino began each day with pro bono writings and invasive interventions that insist and expand upon the first amendment rights of United States citizens. In all areas, he is both knowledgeable and feels national, state, and local governments are stuck in socially immobile positions. He created ways to invade entire cultures and governments to move those stuck in quicksand off the dime and into a society that spirals upward. He refers to the creation of these methods as sanctimonious psychoproctological invasions in the creation of a political psychology that should be studies by all human beings who want to make a difference and give meaning to their lives.

Sanctimonious Psychoproctological Invasions: The Handbook for Political Analysis

Len Bergantino is a multi-faceted individual who achieved international prominence in the areas of psychoanalysis, psychotherapy, clinical psychology, and music. His other fields include education and religion, with a precursory knowledge of medicine and law. He is a weathervane in terms of knowing the right thing to do and has the temperament of Che Guevarra in getting it done!

The Reverend Dr. Len Bergantino, Ed.D. (USC), Ph.D., D. Div. Political Analyst

From 2012 through 2018, Len Bergantino began each day with pro bono writings and invasive interventions that insist and expand upon the first amendment rights of United States citizens. In all areas, he is both knowledgeable and feels national, state, and local governments are stuck in socially immobile positions. He created ways to invade entire cultures and governments to move those stuck in quicksand off the dime and into a society that spirals upward. He refers to the creation of these methods as sanctimonious psychoproctological invasions in the creation of a political psychology that should be studies by all human beings who want to make a difference and give meaning to their lives.

About the Author

Len Bergantino is a multi-faceted individual who achieved international prominence in the areas of psychoanalysis, psychotherapy, clinical psychology, and music. His other fields include education and religion, with a precursory knowledge of medicine and law. He is a weathervane in terms

of knowing the right thing to do and has the temperament of Che Guevarra in getting it done!

ISBN: 978-1-6461-0238-9 • $xx.xx

SAMPLE

9 780805 995510

ROSEDOG BOOKS
585 Alpha Dr, Pittsburgh, PA 15238

Dorrance Publishing Company

Books that are either published or will be published authored by **Dr. Len Bergantino** as these books were written as the thing-in itself and were divinely inspired by the Holy Spirit to at the very least give men and women an opportunity to be more fully themselves and more in touch with their own nature. It is strongly recommended that the readers develop their level of attention to read all four books and permit them to become part parcel of how each individual answers the question "TO BE OR NOT TO BE". As The Reverend Dr. Len Bergantino is seventy five years old, he will not be around personally to do psychoanalysis or psychotherapy with you, therefore these books were written on the basis of them being around for at least TWO HUNDRED YEARS!!!

1. I AM FREUD! Psychoanalysis Is the Only Method of Cure: It's Too Bad No One Knows How to Do One!!!
2. Reverse Analysis, the Existential Shift, Gestalt Family Therapy and the Prevention of the Next Holocaust
3. The Art of Psychotherapy and the Liberation of the Therapist
4. The Essence of Music
5. When Baseball was King The New York Yankees were King of Baseball
6. Germans – Jews – Holocausts and the Collective Unconscious
7. Political Psychology Invasions
8. The Sanctimonious Psychoproctological Invasions: The Handbook for Political Analysis
9. The Denial of Reverse Racism in America
10. The Greatest Basketball Player I Ever Saw

Letter from Pope Francis

Dr. LEN BERGANTINO, Ed.D.(USC), Ph.D., A.B.P.P.

Psychoanalysis

(424) 293-9511

Dear Billionaire,

I WANT YOU TO GIVE A GIFT OF ABOUT TWO MILLION DOLLARS AS A TAX WRITEOFF MUCH AS STIPENDS WERE GIVEN TO MICHAELANGELO FOR PAINTING THE CISTENE CHAPEL! ALONG WITH THIS GIFT AS MY BENEFACTOR IT IS PARAMOUNT THAT YOU FIND THE BEST SYSTEM THAT MARKETS AND DISTRIBUTES BOOKS AND GIVE THEM WHATEVER THEY WANT TO PUT IN BOOKSTORES ON DISPLAY SIX BOOKS I HAVE PUBLISHED BETWEEN NOVEMBER, 2018 AND DECEMBER, 2019.

While it is tantamount to PROVING THE EXISTENCE OF GOD ANY AND ALL BOOKS WILL BE SHIPPED TO YOU UPON REQUEST FOR THIS TAX WRITEOFF!!! (UP TO SIX BOOKS FOR DONOR EVALUATION PURPOSES)

MY BOOKS ARE A PUBLIC SERVICE IN THAT THEY WILL TURN A DOWNWARD SPIRALING SOCIETY INTO AN U PWARD SPIRALING SOCIETY WHEN READ AN INGESTED EN TOTO!

The pages that follow give the billionaire of front and back book covers of how one can develop and utilize '"HIGHER SENSE PERCEPTION IN THE DEVELOPMENT OF LIFE PURSUITS TO AN ART FORM!!!

LEST THERE REMAIN A DEARTH OF QUALITY AND EXCELLENCE THE TAX WRITEOFF OF THE BILLIONAIRE WILL PROVIDE A DEVELOPMENT IN THE HIGHEST CALIBRE OF PERSONS AND CITIZENS FOR AT LEAST THE NEXT TWO HUNDRED YEARS!!! PLEASE READ ON AND CALL BY LETTING 424-293-9511 RING TEN TIMES TO LEAVE A MESSAGE WITH A CALL BACK #!

Sincerely,

Dr. Len Bergantino, Ed.D., Ph.D.

1215 Brockton Ave., Ste. 104, W. Los Angeles, CA 90025-U.S.A.

Dr. LEN BERGANTINO, Ed.D.(USC), Ph.D., A.B.P.P.

Psychoanalysis

(424) 293-9511

November 21, 2019

Dear Psychoanalyst,

I want you to be on the lookout for a book recently sent by my publisher entitled I AM FREUD! PSYCHOANALYSIS IS THE ONLY METHOD OF CURE! IT'S TOO BAD NO ONE KNOWS HOW TO DO ONE!!!

THIS BOOK AND OTHERS I HAVE WRITTEN WILL HELP PSYCHOANALYSTS BECOME "HIGHER SENSITIVES" (as written about in a book in 1967 by Shaffica Karagulla, DeVorss Press). This will make all the difference in successfully working through transferences.

My first book, PSYCHOTHERAPY, INSIGHT AND STYLE: THE EXISTENTIAL MOMENT, 1981 Allyn & Bacon, 1994 retitled MAKING AN IMPACT IN THERAPY: HOW MASTER CLINICIANS INTERVEWE, Jason Aronson, Inc. is an important preface in that the psychoanalytic chapter actually has interviews with the best of Wilfred Bion's Analysands-Supervising and Training Analysts — M.D.'s as well as the order in which Bion's books must be read to develop the level of attention required for psychoanalysis to, in "good faith" continue to grow as a profession! Analysts thought Bion's work was brilliant conceptually and theoretically but not relevant to the practice of psychoanalysis. This IS NOT TRUE AND I AM FREUD, THE BOOK IT TOOK ME FORTY YEARS TO WRITE, DEMONSTRATES MANY OF HIS UNIQUE TECHNICAL APPROACHES TIED TO THE QUALITY OF BEING OF THE PSYCHOANALYST.

FURTHUR, BION SAID "THE ENTIRE PSYCHOANALYTIC LIBRARY IS GOOD for about the first hour and one half of an Analysis) After that YOU HAVE TO KNOW WHAT TO SAY TO THE PATIENT!" Martin Grotjahn,MD told me "Psychoanalysis is a great method of education, but it is ineffective as a method of treatment!"

My also new book "The Art of Psychotherapy And The Liberation of The Therapist" remedies both the concerns of Bion and Grotjahn! As I was trained by 17 or more world renown psychiatrists, psychoanalysts and clinical psychologists THIS UPDATED VERSION OF FORTY YEARS OF THE EXISTENTIAL MOMENT PROVIDES BOTH OPTIONS OF WHAT YOU SAY TO A PATIENT THAT MUST BE INCORPORATED INTO PSYCHOANALYTIC EDUCATION IN WAYS THAT PROVIDE EFFECTIVE TREATMENT! LOOK AT IT THIS WAY! FOR $300,000 OVER A 7 YEAR PERIOD OF FIVE DAY A WEEK ANALYSIS THE PATIENT HAS A RIGHT TO COME OUT OF THE ANALYSIS NOT AS CRAZY AS THE DAY THEY WENT IN!

Sincerely,

P.S. I AM THE ONLY ONE WHO COULD ACTUALLY DO ALL OF WHAT WILFRED BION WROTE!

Dr. Len Bergantino, Ed.D. (USC), Ph.D.,A.B.P.P.

1215 Brockton Ave., Ste. 104, W. Los Angeles, CA 90025-U.S.A.

LEN BERGANTINO, Ed.D., Ph.D., A.B.P.P.

Psychoanalysis
(310) 207-9397

Clinical Psychologist

A.B.P.P. – Diplomate in Family Psychology
American Board of Professional Psychology

DO YOU THINK THAT SOME SLUG WHO LOOKS VERY PROFESSIONAL WHO "WHISPERS" AN OCCASIONAL INTERPRETATION TO YOU FIVE TIMES A WEEK FOR 7 YEARS CAN MAKE ONE BIT OF DIFFERENCE IN YOUR LIFE OR DOES SUCH A PSYCHOTOXIC SLUG CALLED A PSYCHOANALYST MERELY STICK YOU IN AN EMOTIONAL TOILET BOWL FOR SEVEN YEARS HAVING THE CUMULATIVE RESULT OF TURNING YOU INTO A HOPELESS BASTARD WHO WILL NEVER TURN THE TRAGIC CORNER IN HIS OR HER LIFE?

CAN YOUR ANALYST ANALYZE AN ARCHAIC LIQUID SYMBIOTIC OR AN OSMOTIC TRANSFERENCE, OR CAN THEY EVEN RECOGNIZE THIS PHENOMENA IN ORDER TO ANALYZE IT.?! IF THE PSYCHOANALYST CANNOT ANALYZE THESE TRANSFERENCES THEY CAN'T DO AN ANALYSIS!!!

I USED TO GET "GOOD FAITH" PATIENTS WHO HAD THE BALLS TO WORK ON THE CUTTING EDGE AT THE SAME TIME I DID BECAUSE THEY HAD HAD COMBINATIONS OF TWENTY YEARS OF TWO SEVEN YEAR ANALYSES PLUS SEVERAL BRIEFER PSYCHOTHERAPIES, ONLY TO BE AS CRAZY AS THE DAY THEY WALKED IN!!! (-$200,000.00)

AS DR. DONALD RINSLEY, M.D., FELLOW-AMERICAN COLLEGE OF PSYCHOANALYSTS WROTE ABOUT ME, MY WORK HAS BOTH A HEALING EFFECT AND AFFECT. PATIENTS USED TO PAY ME SIX MONTHS IN ADVANCE TO HOLD THE TIME OPEN BECAUSE I WAS IRREPLACEABLE: I WAS THE ONLY ONE WHO COULD ANALYZE THE PSYCHOTIC CORE OF THE PERSONALITY AND I WAS THE ONLY ONE WHO COULD ACTUALLY DO WHAT DR. WILFRED R. BION, MRCS (MEDICAL ROYAL COLLEGE OF SURGEONS) WROTE ABOUT ANALYZING THE PSYCHOTIC CORE OF THE PERSONALITY.

AS I AM SEVENTY SIX YEARS OLD, I HAVE WRITTEN FIVE BOOKS THAT MUST BE READ AND DIGESTED IN THEIR ENTIRETY. AS THESE BOOKS ARE THE THING-IN-ITSELF THEY WILL TRANSFORM THE READER INTO THE KINDS OF ANALYST, PATIENT AND PSYCHOTHERAPIST WHO CAN MAKE A DIFFERENCE IN HELPING PEOPLE TURN THE TRAGIC CORNER IN THEIR LIVES! IN OTHER WORDS, THESE FIVE BOOKS ARE ANALYSIS!

THESE BOOKS WERE WRITTEN TO BE AROUND FOR A FEW HUNDRED YEARS AND WERE DIRECTLY GUIDED BY THE ALMIGHTY!!!

From the Vatican, 17 June 2019

Dear Mr Bergantino,

His Holiness Pope Francis has received your letter, and he has asked me to thank you.

The Holy Father will remember you in his prayers, and he invokes upon you God's blessings of joy and peace.

Yours sincerely,

Monsignor Paolo Borgia
Assessor

Mr Len Bergantino
1215 Brockton Avenue
Suite 104
Los Angeles, CA 90025
USA

The Author

Dr. Len Bergantino, Ed.D., Ph.D.

The Reverend Dr. Len Bergantino was trained in psychoanalysis including the paranormal and ordinary methods of training by Dr. Wilfred R. Biom. MCRS- Medical Royal College of Surgeons. Many of Bion's M.D. Analysands in Beverly Hills, CA, Dr. Martin Grotjahn, M.D. and Dr. Bruno Bettelheim, Ph.D. who was in Freud's original training group. They were all Training Analysts. Dr. Michael Paul M.D. is one of the two best of Bion's Training Analysands.

Dr. Donald Rinsley M.D., Fellow American College of Psychoanalysts wrote about me, "There is no doubt that some people possess a healing capacity and that others do not". "Envies ——jelousies — outsiderism".

A Review

By DONALD B. RINSLEY, M.D., F.R.S.H.,
Fellow, American College of Psychoanalysts;
Fellow, American Psychiatric Association

Psychotherapy, Insight and Style.
By Len Bergantino, Ed.D., Ph.D.
Boston: Allyn and Bacon, 1981, 288 pp.
Published in Bulletin of the Menninger Clinic,
Vol. 47, No. 5, September 1983.

There is no doubt that some people possess a healing capacity
and that others do not; nor is there any doubt that a Zulu witch
doctor, a Puerto Rican curandero, a Navaho medicine man or a
voodoo spiritist may remit symptoms more effectively than the
best trained psychotherapist or psychoanalyst. The differences
between healing and therapy are not inconspicuous even as both
may readily dissolve into quackery in the hands of the exploitive
and the unscrupulous. A wise Freud once commented that the
function of psychoanalysis is to convert neurotic misery into
ordinary human suffering, a point of view to be dismissed only at
one's peril even though it doubtless reflected the essence of
Freud's depressive personality. From such few considerations as
these emerge questions concerning the differences separating
healing and therapy, the features that unite them and the goals
and objectives they may be noted to share. And whatever
answers to these questions may satisfy those who propound
them will reflect whether one's Weltanschauung considers the
world to be a vale of tears or, after the fashion of the Gallic
optimist, Coué, a place where everything keeps getting better
and better.

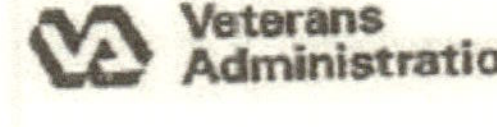

Veterans
Administration

1 July 1985

Len Bergantino, Ed.D., Ph.D.
10266 Kilrenney Avenue
Los Angeles, California 90064

Dear Len:

How nice to receive yours of June 24th, and to
learn of your upward spiral! I'm very pleased indeed
to believe that my little review of your book has
contributed to your success!

Frankly, Len, I have long been eructatively fed
up with the sort of territorial cupidities and other
evidences of narcissistic nonsensicality so many of
the colleagues display. Such antics reveal the essentially limbic nature of people as it comes to be
expressed in envies and jealousies to which you allude in your letter. When I read your book I knew
at once of your outsider-ism (cf. Colin Wilson's
seminal book of the same name—The Outsider) as well
as your talent; since I know I am good also, I do
not need to do the Big-Daddy-in-Cat-On-A-Hot-Tin-
Roof bit, viz., to shit on one's sons out of envy
and fear that they will appropriate my penis-cum-
wife-cum-everything-else!

I trust your family are in good health. Keep
in touch.

Most sincerely,

Donald B. Rinsley, M.D., F.R.S.E. (Lond.)
Associate Chief for Education
Psychiatry Service

Clinical Professor of Psychiatry
University of Kansas School of Medicine
Kansas City

DBR:mtf

The Books

I AM FREUD! Psychoanalysis Is the Only Method of Cure:

It's Too Bad No One Knows How to Do One!!!

This is a book for all time. As I had extrasensory perception to help me find out things on a primitive level and depth with an ability to pick up split-off, severe pathological projective identifications moment to moment in an era when psychologists were only permitted to be research psychoanalysts by the American Psychoanalytic Association (but tightly controlled where that research was going that in many ways nullified it as true psychoanalytic research), I present to you a book that might at that time have been considered wild psychoanalysis. And I will show you how extrasensory perception can be developed and utilized by the therapeutic use of self within the psychoanalytic frame in ways that can enhance the treatment of borderline, narcissistic, obsessive-compulsive, and schizophrenic disorders and other diagnoses, as well as help pinpoint psychophysiological awareness, which through the repetition compulsion, can prevent disease and will circumvent disease in later life. This kind of psychoanalysis will go a long way in preventing the next holocoust!

ORDER A COPY NOW!

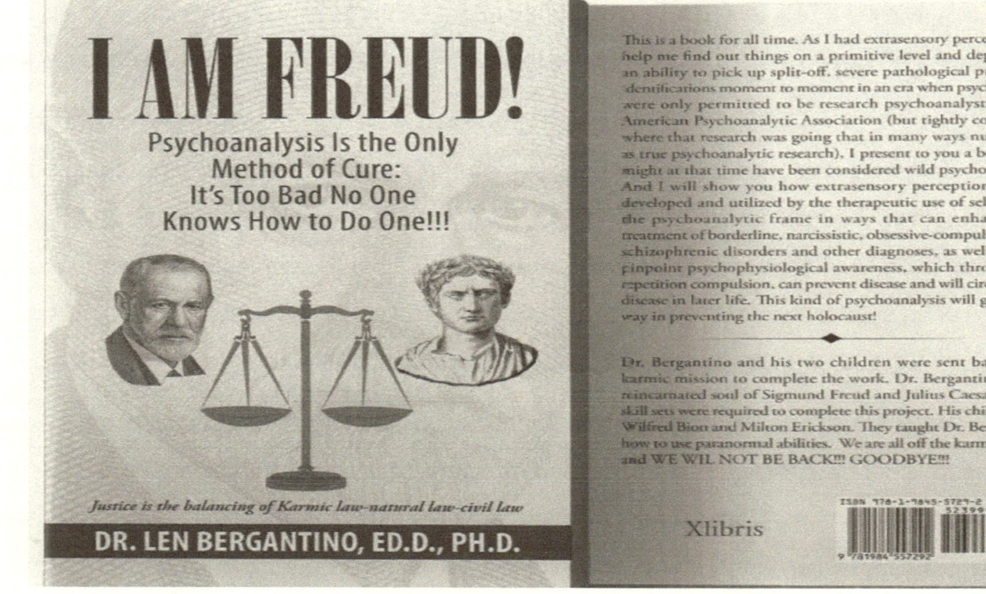

I DARED TO DISTURB THE UNIVERSE!!!

Dr. Len Bergantino Ed. D., Ph.D., releases 'I AM Freud! Psychoanalysis Is the Only Method of Cure: It's Too Bad No One Knows How to Do One!!!"

BEVERLY HILLS, Calif. – Dr. Len Bergantino, Ed.D., Ph.D., is the reincarnated soul of Sigmund Freud and Julius Caesar and his children Lisa Francesca is the reincarnated soul of the great British psychoanalyst Wilfred R. Bion and Cleopatra while his developmentally delayed son Alexander Leonardo is the reincarnated soul of Milton H. Erickson, M.D. (known as the father of Modern Medical Hypnosis and for Uncommon Therapy) and Decimus Brutus. All of those skill sets were necessary in the writing of "I Am Freud! Psychoanalysis Is the Only Method of Cure: It's Too Bad No One Knows How to Do One!!!" (published by Xlibris) and the issues it is meant to deal with at both conscious and unconscious levels.

Furthur, Bergantino in 1980, made a direct contact with God to have Bion and Erickson sent back as the reincarnated souls of his children to teach him what to do with the paranormal gifts that were given to him and unleashed by Erickson. Through this development, he, with God's tutelage became the best psychoanalyst that ever lived and began to implement Freud's plan that both psychoanalysis and subsequently developed psychotherapies would create the kind of patients who would and could then go out and create an upward spiraling society.

Wilhelm Reich, M.D. – Freud's most gifted training analyst said "If you can't do politics, you can't do analysis!" The book shows how to develop extrasensory perception so that analysts and therapists have an opportunity to develop the tools necessary to do the jobs at hand if they are so inclined. In this way, people will not pay for a five day a week, seven year analysis and come out as crazy as the day they began with few if any tools to carry on the work. "When I did an analysis with the crème de la crème of society, they customarily tripled their income and the quality of their life! (Don't waste $50,000 per year or $350,000 per analysis)."

The book is not based on anything Bergantino may or may not believe. It is based on his attaining a level of "pure being" that Jean Paul Sartre wrote about as the thing-in-itself. And it is at that level that this book was written as the thing-in-itself to effect change in the reader.

"I Am Freud! Psychoanalysis Is the Only Method of Cure: It's Too Bad No One Knows How to Do One!!!"

By Dr. Len Bergantino, Ed.D., Ph.D.

Hardcover | 6 x 9in | 504 pages | ISBN 9781984557308

Softcover | 6 x 9in | 504 pages | ISBN 9781984557292

E-Book | 504 pages | ISBN 9781984557285

Available at www.amazon.com and www.barnesandnoble.com

About the Author

Dr. Len Bergantino, Ed.D., Ph.D. practiced psychoanalysis in Beverly Hills, California from 1979-1991. He saw seven patients five days a week for between five and seven years totaling 49 hours a week and saw an occasional family therapy or clinical hypnosis case totaling 52 hours a week at $125 per hour; $625 per week; $240,000 per year. In addition, he trained psychiatrists and clinical psychologists at the international level delivering on his workshop promise "The Therapheutic Wizardry of Dr. Len Bergantino" at Wentworth Castle in Sheffield, England and training the British at the Royal College of Medicine in London in "Developing the Use of Extrasensory Perception in the Practice of Psychoanalysis, Psychotherapy and Clinical Hypnosis." In Brisbane, Australia, his work was described as "a kind of mental precision" that electrified the Australian Therapeutic Community and had lasting therapeutic impact. Furthermore, he was an affiliate of the Italian American Lawyers Association for seven years. He became an expert witness in both severe parental Alienation Syndrome in criminal cases. He was the only clinician to plea bargain a man for release who was on death row. He was President of the Southern California Society of

Clinical Hypnosis when they were composed of exclusively MD's, PHD's and DDS'. The year he was president he turned it into a psychoanalytic institute.

Reverse Analysis, the Existential Shift, Gestalt Family Therapy and the Prevention of the Next Holocaust

The purpose of this book is to tell stories that both entertain and bring value to people's lives. The order of the stories told will have no rhyme or reason other than they went through my unconscious mind when I sat down at the typewriter along with the notion they may have value and reach the unconscious minds of the readers in a way that has a better than average chance of entertaining the reader. As I am seventy-five years old when beginning this book, I have worn many hats during my lifetime, and the stories run the gamut.

REVERSE ANALYSIS, THE EXISTENTIAL SHIFT, GESTALT FAMILY THERAPY AND THE PREVENTION OF THE NEXT HOLOCAUST

Dr. Len Bergantino, Ed.D., Ph.D.

The purpose of this book is to open up the space so that the reader – society at large, psychotherapists and patients might start contributing to LIFE FORCE AND THE THERAPEUTIC USE OF SELF IN CREATING A SOCIETY THAT IS UPWARD SPIRALING INSTEAD OF ONE DOMINATED BY INCURABLE DEATH FORCE! FOR THIS TO HAPPEN SOCIETY AT LARGE MUST LEARN TO THINK AND PAY ATTENTION TO THE FACTS IN THIS BOOK THAT WILL PERMIT THE CREATION OF NEW THOUGHT TO MEET NEW PROBLEMS; SO THAT WE DO NOT HAVE SITUATIONS LIKE 122 VETERANS A DAY COMMITTING SUICIDE WITHOUT HOPE THAT THERE ARE ANY TREATMENTS FOR THEM NOW OR THAT CAN BE CREATED! IT IS RECOMMENDED THAT THIS BOOK BE READ AS ONE OF A SERIES OF FOUR WRITTEN BY DR. LEN BERGANTINO TO CREATE THIS NEW SOCIETY! WHILE PSYCHOTHERAPY IS THE MEDIUM OF CHOICE IN TH THIS BOOK, THE FOURTH BOOK UTILIZES MUSIC AS THE MEDIUM TO ANSWER SHAKESPEARE'S QUESTIONS "TO BE OR NOT TO BE!!!!!!!!!!!!!!!!!!!!!!!!!!!!!!!"

My Children and I were sent back on a karmic mission to PREVENT THE APOCALYPSE AND WE HAVE DONE OUR PART IN WRITING FOUR BOOKS. NOW IT IS UP TO YOU TO READ AND UTILIZE THEM! GOD HAS MYSTERIOUSLY MURDERED THREE PERSONS WHO COULD HAVE STOPPED ME FROM FULFILLING THIS MISSION! WE HAVE SUCCEEDED! THE REST IS UP TO YOU OR YOUR ROOMS WILL BE RESERVED IN HELL! Twelve out of 100 million make it into Heaven!

Xlibris

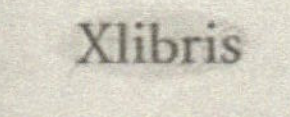

ISBN 978-1-7960-2117-2
51999
9 781796 021172

"This book is a one-session existential shift in a lifelong personality characteristic of a patient"

The Art of Psychotherapy and the Liberation of the Therapist

This is a book for professional psychotherapists, psychoanalysts and counselors, students in those areas of specialty and laypersons who are interested in the essence of effective therapy and how some of the people who do it best practice their art. For professionals, the book presents a personal way of viewing therapy that can add pleasurable options. Each of the therapists with whom Bergantino worked, and himself, all had a feeling of enjoyment that they hope will carry over to the office and practices of the readers. For students of therapy, the book offers a search for a professional stature and working posture that may be of value in the development of each student's unique personal style. For laypersons, the book speaks of therapy that can make an impact and speaks of how some of the most potent therapists practice.

The Art of
Psychotherapy
And the Liberation
of the Therapist

Much has been written about the Science of Psychotherapy, but it has remained for Dr. Bergantino to write about the Art of Psychotherapy with such elegant impact.

Dr. Len Bergantino, Ed.D., Ph.D.

This is a book for professional psychotherapists, psychoanalysts, and counselors; students in those areas of specialty; and lay persons who are interested in the essence of effective therapy and how some of the people who do it best practice their art. For professionals, the book presents a personal way of viewing therapy that can add pleasurable options. Each of the therapists with whom I worked, and myself, all had a feeling of enjoyment that we hope will carry over to the office and practices of the readers. For students of therapy, the book offers a search for a professional stature and working posture that may be of value in the development of each student's unique personal style. For lay persons, the book speaks of therapy that can make an impact and speaks of how some of the most potent therapists practice. For Psychoanalysts interested in the work of the Great British Psychoanalyst, Dr. Wilfred R. Bion MRCS (Medical Royal College of Surgeons), This is the only book that demonstrates exactly what he did.

I wrote the book with the intention of having it be both an experience and an explanation. I have presented it according to my developmental needs while maturing personally and professionally. This was done so the book might be informative at the conscious level, entertaining at the child level, and persuasive at the unconscious level.

The existential moment is the thread that ties the book together; it is a moment of therapeutic potency. While all moments are existential by definition, there are certain moments that are more powerful in helping patients live happier and healthier lives. Positive results, whether they be from one session or over the long haul, are partially, if not fully, a result of existential moments.

Xlibris

ISBN 978-1-7960-2422-7
52399
9 781796 024227

The Essence of Music

This multi-purpose book serves as a natural model for how musicians, as human beings, deal with each other. It provides a baseline for humans in answering Shakespeare's question, "To be or not to be." Furthermore, the book is substantive and full of depth, enough to be used in music schools no matter what musical genre since it focuses on musicality, pure sound, the art of musicality and peace. It can be utilized in the psychotherapeutic arts, and its content is healing in nature.

The Essence of Music will teach you the ingredients required "TURN NOTES INTO MUSIC!"

Music is the international language, but what is music!?!?

For The Bergantino-Bredice Family Music was the FAMILY BUSINESS!
My father, Dan Bergantino, always told me, (in terms of what kind of music you listen to) "IF YOU PUT SHIT IN, SHIT WILL COME OUT! (WHEN YOU PLAY MUSIC)

My cousin Louis Bredice told me, "When I first started playing Jazz, I played a lot of notes! Then I realized, all I needed were the right ones!"

My cousin Freddie Bredice had the fastest technique on guitar I had ever seen! The first time I met him was on a gig in 1967. His speed was blinding, faster than a speeding bullet! I was leaning against a wooden beam next to him and when he finished I said, "You must be cousin Fred!" He said, "Yeah, I don't play chords! It fucks up your hands! "Freddie was one of Joe Diorio's guitar teachers and Joe said he still has nightmares about Freddie's speed! Joe was known as the best jazz guitar playerin the world among guitar players. I got him to play songs again in a cd entitled "FALLING IN LOVE" where I am playing mandolin and Joe is accompanying me on guitar. This cd can be purchased from orchard records.com and amazon.com . On the top picture: LISA BERGANTINO (left), DR. LEN BERGANTINO (middle), and ALEX BERGANTINO (right).

This is a multi-purpose book in that much as a previously published book entitled "ZEN AND THE ART OF MOTORCYCLE MAINTENANCE" had more to do with human growth than motorcycle maintenance; this book is a natural model of how musicians as human beings deal with each other thereby providing a baseline for humans in answering Shakespeare's question, "TO BE OR NOT TO BE!" FURTHER, THIS BOOK IS SUBSTANTIVE AND DEPTHFUL ENOUGH TO BE USED IN MUSIC SCHOOLS, NO MATTER WHAT MUSIC GENRE, IN THAT IT FOCUSES ON MUSICALITY, PURE SOUND, THE ART OF MELODY AND PEACE" AND IT CAN BE UTILIZED IN THE PSYCHOTHERAPEUTIC ARTS AND ITS CONTENTS ARE HEALING IN NATURE!

THE REVEREND DR. LEN BERGANTINO
PROFESSIONAL MUSICIAN FROM 1996-2012
(AGE 56-70) MUSICIAN'S LOCAL 47
AMERICAN FEDERATION OF MUSICIAN'S

Xlibris

On the bottom picture:
HARRY JAMES - 1942

ISBN 978-1-7960-2916-1
51999
9 781796 029161

When Baseball was King The New York Yankees were King of Baseball

Dr. Len Bergantino's most intense love affair with baseball was between the years 1951 – 1961. Then he went to college and his attentions went elsewhere. Yet, he returned to baseball by reading baseball books on overseas flights and noticed that every time he read about baseball, it brought peace and tranquility to his life. This prompted him to pen **When Baseball was King The New York Yankees were King of Baseball**.

*THE MINIMUM CONDITIONS REQUIRED TO ACHIEVE THE COMPLETE DEVELOPMENT OF YOUR OWN BEING REQUIRES THAT YOU READ EACH OF THE BOOKS IN A MANNER WHERE THE WORK IS INTEGRATED AT A DEEP AND SUBSTANTIVE LEVEL. THE BASEBALL BOOK ROUNDS OUT THE CHILDHOOD FUN ASPECTS OF YOUR PERSONAL DEVELOPMENT.

When Baseball was King
The New York Yankees were
King of Baseball

Dr. Len Bergantino, Ed.D., Ph.D.

This photo was given to me by the Mick himself. (Courtesy of Mickey Mantle)

The Reverend Dr. Len Bergantino is a multi-faceted individual who achieved international prominence in the areas of psychoanalysis, psychotherapy, clinical psychology, and music. His other fields include education and religion, with a precursory knowledge of medicine and law. He is a weathervane in terms of knowing the right thing to do and has the temperament of Che Guevarra in getting it done!

When the Reverend Dr. Len Bergantino grew up, the first thing he had in mind was to wear number 22 and take over for Alfie Reynolds, the Super Chief, as the Mainstay of the Mound Staff of the NEW YORK YANKEES!!! The New York Yankees won 5-world series in a row. (1949-1953) !!!

Xlibris

ISBN 978-1-7960-7891-6
51599

This photo was given to me by Mick himself. (Courtesy of Mickey Mantle)

This book is comprised of methods and stories that are intended to evoke a one session existential shift in the reader's grasp of the entire situation in a way that supplants the word "appropriate" with the words "finer and finer discriminations of pure being" and the addition of the words "creative aggression" as an authentic working tool!

Sincerely,

Dr. Len Bergantino, Ed.D., Ph.D.

Author Dr. Len Bergantino, Ed.D., writes letters that are addressed to editors, professors and some of the known political figures such as Senator Bernie Sanders, Congresswoman Tulsi Gabbard, Senator Sheila Keuhl, Chancellor Angela Merkel of Germany, Queen Elizabeth, President Donald Trump. He expresses his stands on some issues using psychological perspective in an honest and conversational way as possible.

Excerpt taken from the conclusion section of the book:

This book has nothing to do with the politics of the word "appropriate" and how those that read it may try to spin it. This book has everything to do with the primitive nature of man and what is actually required to educate peoples of all countries from all walks of life, no matter what caste system they knowingly or unknowingly are stuck in! Along the way to my training family therapists at the international level, Dr. Carl Whitaker, M.D., my teacher and mentor from 1979- 1994, in his last verbal communication to me said, "the work is easy! It's the justification that is hard!" So I will merely present you the facts as they occurred. I will provide no justification for any of it, other than to tell you that is what really occurred in an American system of education between 1949 and 1996 and much of it was unexpected and rather shocking to me.

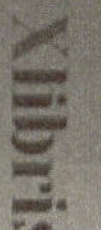

POLITICAL PSYCHOLOGY
INVASIONS
DR. LEN BERGANTINO, Ed.D., Ph.D.

ISBN 978-1-7960-8444-3
9 781796 084443
51999

Xlibris

"POLITICAL PSYCHOLOGY INVASIONS"

This book focuses upon the initial psycho-political assessments of the Democratic candidates who were among the sixteen original characters that threw their "hats in the ring!" so to speak! Further, it shows those interested in the current political climate and all other historical political climates HOW TO DIFFERENTIATE REAL NEWS FROM FAKE NEW THROUGH THE DEVELOPMENT AND UTILIZATION OF HIGHER SENSE PERCEPTION.

THE BOOK FURTHER INVADES SEVERAL POLITICAL AND RELIGIOUS TERRITORIES N DEMONSTRATING "HOW TO ASSESS AND DO THE RIGHT THING" AS A WAY OF LIFE, THEREBY AS CITIZENS HELPING TO CREATE AN UPWARD AS OPPOSED TO A DOWNWARD SPIRALING SOCIETY.

IN ADDITION TO ASSESSING AND MAKING DIRECT RECOMMENDATIONS TO THE POPE, AS WELL AS POLITICIANS DIRECT RECOMMENDATIONS ARE MADE SUCH AS THE DOING AWAY WITH LICENSING BOARDS IN THE FIELDS OF PSYCHOANALYSIS, CLINICAL PSYCHOLOGY, PSYCHOTHERAPY, MARITAL AND FAMILY THERAPY AND CLINICAL SOCIAL WORK SO AS NOT TO PROVIDE:

THE GENERAL PUBLIC A FALSE SENSE OF SECURITY WHILE ACTUALLY DESTROYING CLINICIANS" ABILITY TO DO THE WORK THAT CAN ONLY COME WITH THE EVER GROWING THERAPEUTIC USE OF SELF -OR AS SHAKESPEARE UT IT, "TO BE OR NOT TO BE!"

Submitted by Dr. Len   Bergantino, Ed.D., Ph.D.

The Sanctimonious Psychoproctological Invasions: The Handbook for Political Analysis

From 2012 through 2018, Len Bergantino began each day with pro bono writings and invasive interventions that insist and expand upon the first amendment rights of United States citizens. In all areas, he is both knowledgeable and feels national, state, and local governments are stuck in socially immobile positions. He created ways to invade entire cultures and governments to move those stuck in quicksand off the dime and into a society that spirals upward. He refers to the creation of these methods as sanctimonious psychoproctological invasions in the creation of a political psychology that should be studies by all human beings who want to make a difference and give meaning to their lives.

Publisher: Dorrance Publishing Co

To Order a copy of The Sanctimonious Psychoproctological Invasions (ISBN 978-1-6461-0238-9)

Email: bookorders@rosedogbooks.com

Or call 1-800-788-7654 (Mon-Fri) 9AM-4PM

The Denial of Reverse Racism in America

Do you think that some slug who looks very professional who "whispers" an occasional interpretation to you five times a week for 7 years can make one bit of difference in your life or does such a psychotoxic slug called a psychoanalyst merely stick you in an emotional toilet bowl for seven years having the cumulative result of turning you into a hopeless bastard who will never turn the tragic corner in his or her life?

Can your analyst analyze an archaic liquid symbiotic or an osmotic transference, or can they even recognize this phenomena in order to analyze it? If the psychoanalyst cannot analyze these transferences they can't do an analysis!

I used to get "good faith" patients who had the balls to work on the cutting edge at the same time I did because they had had combinations of twenty years of two seven year analyses plus several briefer psychotheraphies, only to be as crazy as the day they walked in! (-$200,000.00)

As Dr. Donald Rinsley, M.D., fellow-American College of Psychoanalysts wrote about me, my work has both a healing effect and affect. Patients used to pay me six months in advance to hold the time open because I was irreplaceable; I was the only one who could analyze the psychotic core of the personality and I was the only who could actually do what Dr. Wilfred R. Bion, MRCS (Medical Royal College of Surgeons) wrote about analyzing the psychotic core of the personality/

As I am seventy-six years old, I have written five books that must be read and digested in their entirety. As these books are the thing-in-itself they will transform the reader into the kinds of analyst, patient and psychotherapist who can make a difference in helping people turn the tragic corner in their lives! In other words, these five books are analysis!

These books were written to be around for a few hundred years and were directly guided by the Almighty!

PRESS RELEASE FOR "THE DENIAL OF REVERSE RACISM IN AMERICA"

THIS BOOK IS INTENDED TO HELP BLACK PEOPLE – PARTICULARLY THOSE IN ADMINISTRATIVE POSITIONS AT THE TOP FOR TREATING WHITE PEOPLE AT THE BOTTOM OF THE TOTEM POLE WHILE DOING IN THE BEST AND BRIGHTEST OF THEIR OWN BLACK CHILDREN AND FALSELY BLAMING IT ON WHITES so as to provide a psychotic PROTECTION GAME OF BLACKS THAT BOTH DO IN THEIR OWN YOUTH AND NEVER ROLL OVER ON ANY BLACK BROTHER OR SISTER THAT REMINDS THEM OF TWO HUNDRED YEARS OF SLAVERY WHILE AT THE SAME TIME PRETENDING TO BE FAIR BY USING "GUILT" AS A MANIPULATION TO JUSTIFY KEEPING "WHITE BOY" AT THE BOTTOM OF THE SOLUTION IS SIMPLE BUT NOT EASY! "BLACK BOY" THE TOTEM POLE! HAS TO STOP BLAMING AND LAYING "GUILT TRIPS" ON MODERNS "WHITE BOY" FOR HIS FOREFATHERS' SINS!"

THIS NEEDS IMMEDIATE CORRECTION IF "WHITE BOY" IS NOT TO BUILD SUCH PRIMITIVE RESENTMENT AT THE UNCONSCIOUS LEVEL THAT YOU GET ONE NEWSLINE AFTER THE OTHER THAT "WHITE BOY" COP SHOOTS BLACK TWELVE YEAR OLD KID RUNNING AWAY IN THE BACK! THIS BOOK PROVIDES AN INTERIM STEP FOR BOTH BLACKS AND WHITES TO EXAMINE THEIR OWN UNDERLYING RACIAL THOUGHTS AND FEELINGS IN A MANNER THAT BRINGS THE SUBCONSCIOUS AND UNCONSCIOUS MORE TO THE SURFACE IN A WAY THAT HELPS THOSE WHO SO ENDEAVOR TO FIND ONGOING SOLUTIONS TO DEAL WITH THE PRIMITIVE REMNANTS OF CRIMES COMMITTED THROUGH TWO HUNDRED YEARS OF SLAVERY! FOR EXAMPLE, I WAS GETTING DONE IN BY A WAITER IN KOLN, GERMANY OF ITALIAN DESCENT in 1990 IN AN ITALIAN RESTAURANT AND THE OWNER SAID HE HATED AMERICANS BECAUSE GENERAL PATTON KILLED HIS ENTIRE FAMILY WHEN COMING THROUGH ITALY IN 1944!

PRESS RELEASE FOR "THE GREATEST BASKETBALL PLAYER I EVER SAW"

To notice greatness and not deny greatness in others you have to notice details that ordinary people often claim do not exist. As ordinary people would much rather blame the victim rather than do their own personal work of self-development. They often deny greatness in others to protect themselves from looking at their own shortcomings often through "hatred and deceptive manipulation (malevolent omnipotence!) Such was the case with Billy Finn, who were he not surrounded by assholes would have averaged fifty two points a game instead of merely holding the state record of fifty two points in one game!

Greatness Kobe Bryant, Elgin Baylor, Larry Bird, Magic Johnson, Bill Russell, LeBron James are all great and have an element of greatness that I have never seen surpassed in my 77 years. Kobe Bryant and LeBron James came into the national basketball association or NBA as it is called right out of high school.

***When Billy Finn played there was no such option! Bob Cousy, famed guard told him he had nothing to teach him in the seventh grade!

***Billy Finn was to basketball what Willie mays was to baseball – the most exciting ballplayer that ever lived despite elements of greatness in others. For example, Ted Williams was the greatest hitter I ever saw. I saw him take batting practice. He hit consecutive line drives so hard they nearly bounced back to 2nd base. This book lays out the details of what made Billy Finn the greatest basketball player who ever lived!

The Greatest
Basketball Player
I Ever Saw

Len Bergantino

PRESS RELEASE
FOR
"THE GREATEST BASKETBALL PLAYER I EVER SAW"

TO NOTICE GREATNESS AND NOT DENY GREATNESS IN OTHERS YOU HAVE TO NOTICE DETAILS THAT ORDINARY PEOPLE OFTEN CLAIM DO NOT EXIST. AS ORDINARY PEOPLE WOULD MUCH RATHER BLAME THE VICTIM RATHER THAN DO THEIR OWN PERSONAL WORK OF SELF DEVELOPMENT. THEY OFTEN DENY GREATNESS IN OTHERS TO PROTECT THEMSELVES FROM LOOKING AT THEIR OWN SHORTCOMINGS OFTEN THROUGH HATRED AND DECEPTIVE MANIPULATION (MALEVOLENT OMNIPOTENCE) SUCH WAS THE CASE WITH BILLY FINN, WHO WERE HE NOT SURROUNDED BY ASSHOLES YOU COULD HAVE AVERAGED FIFTY TWO POINTS A GAME INSTEAD OF MERELY HOLDING THE STATE RECORD OF FIFTY TWO POINTS IN ONE GAME.

GREATNESS. KOBE BRYANT, ELGIN BAYLOR, LARRY BIRD, MAGIC JOHNSON, BILL RUSSELL, LEBRON JAMES ARE ALL GREAT AND HAVE AN ELEMENT OF GREATNESS THAT I HAVE NEVER SEEN SURPASSED IN MY 75 YEARS. KOBE BRYANT AND LEBRON JAMES CAME INTO THE NATIONAL BASKETBALL ASSOCIATION (NBA) AS IT INSTALLED RIGHT OUT OF HIGH SCHOOL.

WHEN BILLY FINN PLAYED THERE WAS NO SUCH OPTION. BOB COUSY, FAMED GUARD TOLD HIM HE HAD NOTHING TO TEACH HIM IN THE SIXTH GRADE.

BILLY FINN WAS TO BASKETBALL WHAT WILLIE MAYS WAS TO BASEBALL: THE MOST EXCITING BALLPLAYER THAT EVER LIVED DESPITE ELEMENTS OF GREATNESS IN OTHERS. FOR EXAMPLE, TED WILLIAMS WAS THE GREATEST HITTER I EVER SAW. I SAW HIM TAKE BATTING PRACTICE. HE HIT CONSECUTIVE LINE DRIVES SO HARD THEY NEARLY BOUNCED BACK TO 2ND BASE. THIS BOOK EXPLAINS THE DETAILS OF WHAT MADE BILLY FINN THE GREATEST BASKETBALL PLAYER WHO EVER LIVED.

Xlibris

ISBN 978-1-7965-9592-6
52800

SANCTIMONIOUS PSYCHOPROCTOLOGICAL INVASIONIST

MY LAST SUPERVISOR, DR. BRUNO BETTELHEIM, WAS TRAINED IN FREUD'S ORIGINAL TRAINING GROUP. FREUD TOLD HIM THAT "WILHELM REICH, M.D. WAS FREUD'S MOST GIFTED TRAINING ANALYST."

DR. WILHELM REICH SAID, "IF YOU CAN'T DO POLITICS, YOU CAN'T DO ANALYSIS!" DR. BERGANTINO SAYS, "THAT IS THE KIND OF ANALYSIS THAT REACHES AND TRANSFORMS THE UNDERLYING PSYCHOTIC THINKING DISORDERS, PRIMITIVE MENTAL STATES AND PSYCHOTIC CORE OF THE PERSONALITIES OF WHAT ARE THOUGHT TO BE YOUR EVERYDAY NARCISSISTIC, BORDERLINE AND OBSESSIVE COMPULSIVE PERSONALITY DISORDERS!!

Reviews

LEN BERGANTINO, Ed.D., Ph.D., A.B.P.P.

Psychoanalysis
(310) 207-9397

p. 2

Clinical Psychologist

A.B.P.P. - Diplomate in Family Psychology
American Board of Professional Psychology

<u>REVIEWS</u>

"When thinking of all the therapist I have ever trained or seen (including Fritz Perls, M.D., Ph.D.) Bergantino! Him I think about! Him I consider! He is a man of depth! He is a man of substance!"

Dr. Donald Rinsley, M.D., (particularly helpful for The Art of Psychotherapy and the Liberation of the Therapist) wrote, "A unique feature of Dr. Bergantino's presentation -offering FASCINATING AND INSTRUCTIVE INSIGHTS INTO THE THERAPEUTIC LABORS OF ADMITTEDLY GIFTED TREATERS."

Dr. Carl Whitaker, M.D. wrote "The approach to his own craziness, the freedom from the culture bind, and the discipline of self each emerged as obtainable goals of that professional parent we call the psychotherapist."

Psychiatrist Barry Blicharski wrote "I am happy to recommend Len Bergantino as an excellent workshop leader, trainer and psychotherapist...We will be inviting Len Bergantino to return to AUSTRALIA AND I RECOMMEND HIS WORK, BOTH CLINICAL AND TEACHING, IN ANY SITUATION.

Betty Erickson, wife of Milton Erickson, M.D. dictated, "The mutual respect that Dr. Erickson and Dr. Bergantino held for each other was reflected in the friendshop that continued until Dr. Erickson's death..., and has continued with Dr. Erickson's widow, Elizabeth Erickson, now 92 years old."

Yaro Starak, Gestalt Therapy trainer and Director of International Gestalt Therapy Training Institute in Brisbane , Australia said of Dr. Bergantino and the workshops he gave in Australia, "<u>Dr. Bergantino has a mental precision that electrified the Australian therapeutic community and had lasting therapeutic impact.</u>

Clinical Psychologist whose name I cannot locate; "DR. BERGANTINO IS THE MOST GIFTED CLINICIAN OF HIS TIME!"

MY OWN REVIEW

THE MOST GIFTED CLINICIAN OF ALLTIME! THE BEST THAT EVER LIVED! IN ADDITION TO WHAT THE MORTALS HAVE SAID ABOUT ME I HAVE FULFILLED MY KARMIC MISSION AS AGREED UPON AT THE BEGINNING OF MY CAREER OVER A FIFTY TWO YEAR PERIOD OF TIME AND AS CONTINUALLY INTERVENDED UPON BY THE HOLY SPIRIT TO ACCOMPLISH THE TASK ONLY EXPANDED UPON TO INFINITY AS STATED BY Dr. Robert Dorn, M.D. , Training and Supervising Analyst, who state

1215 Brockton Ave., Ste. 104, W. Los Angeles, CA 90025 - U.S.A.

LEN BERGANTINO, Ed.D., Ph.D., A.B.P.P.

Psychoanalysis
(310) 207-9397

p. 1

Clinical Psychologist

A.B.P.P. - Diplomate in Family Psychology
American Board of Professional Psychology

<u>REVIEWS</u>

Dr. Wilfred R. Bion, MRCS (Medical Royal College of Surgeons,) the great British psychoanalyst wrote to Dr. Bergantino, "<u>Your work is evocative and stimulating.</u>"

Dr. Milton H. Erickson, M.D. -the Father of Modern Medical Hypnosis told Dr. Bergantino "<u>I am just an old man who tells stories. It's your unconscious mind that has the pinpoint accuracy.</u>" "<u>I respect your dedication to the work.</u>" And so <u>Reverse Analysis was born along with a working knowledge of The Existential Shift</u>.

Dr. Donald Rinsley, M.D., Fellow of The American College of Psychoanalysts wrote of Dr. Bergantino and his work "There is no doubt that some people possess a healing capacity and that others do not"; "I knew at once of your outsiderism...as well as your talent."

Dr. Carl Whitaker, M.D. - the foremost family therapist at the international level wrote of Dr. Bergantino, and his work, "He is a professional reporter of international change models in the family therapy set and even intrapsychic change process." Reading his work "is an active experience in the use of self in the field of psychotherapy, and as such, it both expands and enriches the community standards of practice of professional psychotherapists."

Dr. James Grotstein, M.D., Training and Supervising Analyst wrote of me, "I finally had the pleasure of viewing your tape. I found it very impressive. It helped me to understand better where you are coming from and to be able to observe first hand your intuitive way of approaching people. <u>Your technique reminded me of an elegant sophistication of Gestalt along with Erickson and Bion.</u>"

Dr. Martin Grotjahn, M.D., Training and Supervising Analyst wrote "Dr. Bergantino is obviously a gifted therapist..Most cases as reported in the literature describe the patient's associations and productions while the therapist remains hidden in the mystery of darkness unrevealed. Dr. B is an exception: the great advantage of his work is the opeess and frankness with which the author reveals his experiences when treating patients or when accepting himself as a patient of another therapist."

Dr. James S. Simkin, Ph.D., -Diplomate-American Board of Professional Psychology said of Dr. Bergantino.

1215 Brockton Ave., Ste. 104, W. Los Angeles, CA 90025 - U.S.A.

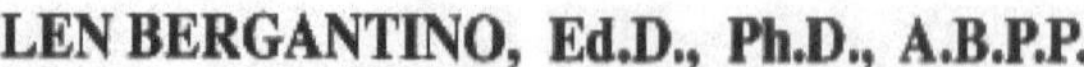

LEN BERGANTINO, Ed.D., Ph.D., A.B.P.P.

Psychoanalysis
(310) 207-9397

Clinical Psychologist

A.B.P.P. - Diplomate in Family Psychology
American Board of Professional Psychology

REVIEWS

WHEN I first started to build my private practice in Beverly Hills,
California. "I think psychoanalysts, psychiatrists and clinical
psychologists have a hard time understanding each other It is like
the Tower of Babel. I think you are the one who can write in a way
whereby they can both understand and talk to each other. Dr. Dorn
wasn't in it for the money. He left Beverly Hills to become Dean
of the Dept. of Psychiatry at Eastern VIrginia Medical School.

I have always loved the BRITS! I gave a workshop in Sheffield,
England at Wentworth Castle entitled "THE THERAPEUTIC
WIZARDRY OF DR. LEN BERGANTINO!" and one at the Royal College of
Medicine entitled "THE DEVELOPMENT AND USE OF EXTRA SENSORY
PERCEPTION IN THE PRACTICE OF PSYCHOANALYSIS, PSYCHOTHERAPY AND
CLINICAL HYPNOSIS". I DELIVERED THE GOODS EACH AND EVERY TIME OUT!

Dr. Len Bergantino, Ed.D., Ph.D.

IN OTHER WORDS WHEN GOD USED THE KARMIC WHEEL TO SEND ME BACK
AS THE REINCARNATED SOULS OF SIGMUND FREUD AND JULIUS CAESAR
AND MY CHILDREN LISA, BACK AS THE REINCARNATED SOULS OF DR.
WILFRED R. BION AND CLEOPATRA AND MY SON ALEX AS THE
REINCARNATED SOULS OF DR. MILTON H. ERICKSON AND BRUTUS,
ASSESSING THAT ALL OF THOSE SKILL SETS WERE NECESSARY TO DO
THE JOB, HOW CAN MY OWN EVALUATION OF ME, MY CLINICAL SKILLS,
AND MY WRITINGS OF ALL FOUR BOOKS BE ANYTHING LESS THAN

I AM THE BEST PSYCHOANALYST OF ALL TIME AND IN ACCORD WITH MY
ORIGINAL IDEA (FREUD -THE LAST TIME AROUND), THE SLOW READING
AND INTEGRATION OF ALL FOUR BOOKS WILL EVOKE AN UPWARD
SPIRALING SOCIETY AND PREVENT BOTH THE NEXT HOLOCAUST AND THE
APOCALIPSE AND FREE FROM THE DESTRUCTION OF THE LINKS TO
KNOWLEDGE AT THE HANDS OF ENVIOUS AND HATEFUL HUMAN MORTAL
COLLEAGUES!

IN OTHER WORDS GOD HAS REVIEWED ME AND MY WORK AND ANYONE ELSE
PALES IN COMPARISON!

1215 Brockton Ave., Ste. 104, W. Los Angeles, CA 90025 - U.S.A.

I Am Freud! Psychoanalysis Is the Only Method of Cure: It's Too Bad No One Knows How to Do One!!!

This book shows how extrasensory perception can be developed, utilized by the therapeutic use of self, and help pinpoint psychophysiological awareness, which can prevent disease and circumvent disease in later life.

www.xlibris.com

ISBN 13 (SOFT): 978-1-9845-5729-2
ISBN 13 (HARD): 978-1-9845-5730-8
ISBN 13 (eBook): 978-1-9845-5728-5

ORDER A COPY NOW!

Reverse Analysis, the Existential Shift, Gestalt Family Therapy and the Prevention of the Next Holocaust

This is a clinical example of a one-session existential shift in a lifelong personality characteristic of a patient. This is for hypnosis or training in hypnosis contact.

www.xlibris.com

ISBN 13 (SOFT): 978-1-7960-2117-2
ISBN 13 (HARD): 978-1-7960-2118-9
ISBN 13 (eBook): 978-1-7960-2116-5

ORDER A COPY NOW!

The Art of Psychotherapy and the Liberation of the Therapist

This is a book for professional psychotherapists, psychoanalysts and counselors, students in those areas of specialty and laypersons who are interested in the essence of effective therapy an how some of the people who do it best practice their art.

www.xlibris.com

ISBN 13 (SOFT): 978-1-7960-2422-7
ISBN 13 (HARD): 978-1-7960-2423-4
ISBN 13 (eBook): 978-1-7960-2421-0

ORDER A COPY NOW!

The Essence of Music

This multi-purpose book serves as a natural model for how musicians, as human beings, deal with each other.

www.xlibris.com

ISBN 13 (SOFT): 978-1-7960-2916-1
ISBN 13 (HARD): 978-1-7960-2917-8
ISBN 13 (eBook): 978-1-7960-2915-4

ORDER A COPY NOW!

When Baseball was King The New York Yankees were King of Baseball

Come and join Dr. Len Bergantino as he recounts and celebrates the glory of The New York Yankees.

www.xlibris.com

ISBN 13 (SOFT): 978-1-7960-7891-6
ISBN 13 (eBook): 978-1-7960-8028-5

ORDER A COPY NOW!

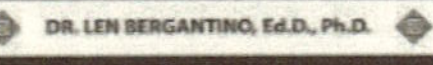

Germans – Jews – Holocausts and the Collective Unconscious

There is no available information at this time. Author will provide once available.

www.xlibris.com

ISBN 13 (SOFT): 978-1-7960-8445-0
ISBN 13 (eBook): 978-1-7960-8446-7

ORDER A COPY NOW!

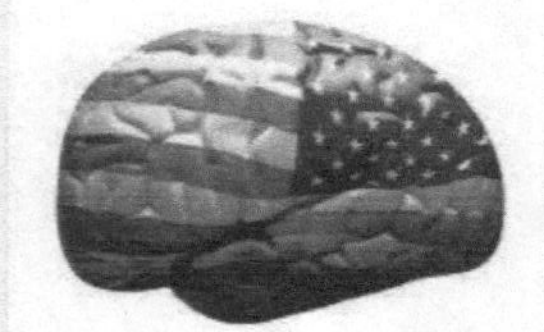

Political Psychology Invasions

See how Dr. Len Bergantino, Ed.D., Ph.D. assess the Democratic candidates in POLITICAL PSYCHOLOGY INVASIONS.

www.xlibris.com

ISBN 13 (SOFT): 978-1-7960-2916-1
ISBN 13 (HARD): 978-1-7960-2917-8
ISBN 13 (eBook): 978-1-7960-2915-4

ORDER A COPY NOW!

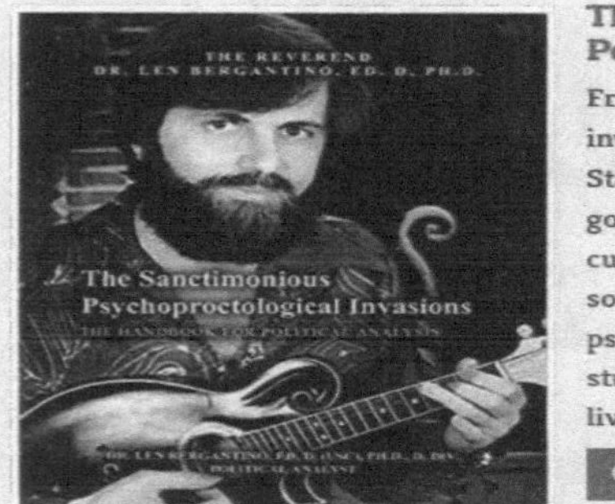

The Sanctimonious Psychoproctological Invasions: The Handbook for Political Analysis

From 2012 through 2018, Len Bergantino began each day with pro bono writings and invasive interventions that insist and expand upon the first amendment rights of United States citizens. In all areas, he is both knowledgeable and feels national, state, and local governments are stuck in socially immobile positions. He created ways to invade entire cultures and governments to move those stuck in quicksand off the dime and into a society that spirals upward. He refers to the creation of these methods as sanctimonious psychoproctological invasions in the creation of a political psychology that should be studies by all human beings who want to make a difference and give meaning to their lives.

ORDER A COPY NOW!

Publisher: Dorrance Publishing Co

To Order a copy of The Sanctimonious Psychoproctological Invasions (ISBN 978-1-6461-0238-9)
Email: bookorders@rosedogbooks.com
Or call 1-800-788-7654 (Mon-Fri) 9AM-4PM

Home | The Author | The Books | Excerpt | Reviews | Order Now

I AM FREUD!

I Am Freud delves deep into the mind of both the psychoanalyst, Sigmund Freud, his psychology practice, and the psychoanalytical process overall. The book introduces the reader to Freud with autobiographical anecdotes and the author's life experience concerning the previous, current, and the future of the discipline, which primarily focuses on the vital political connection of the subject. There are interviews and interactions between the author and Dr. Bettelheim, followed by anecdotes, letters, and notes that draw on Freud's work and the importance of sensory perception in relation to the awakening of the subconscious mind.

This book offered a refreshing view of the complex and immensely interesting findings and perspectives on the psychoanalytical world. It's a great read that discusses subjects in a conversational tone and it's welcoming to beginners on the topic into this complex but fascinating discussion. I found the second section of the book particularly insightful, with more focus on Freud's personality and the impact his nature had on his perception of reality and interactions with his patients. It's clear that the author is passionate about this subject and enthusiastically shares anecdotes and colorful analogies about treating patients in this interesting field of study.

While the book doesn't specifically include specific studies or statistical data on psychology pertaining to Freud's findings, it's a great read that opens discussion on a topic that many people find interesting. *I Am Freud* by Dr. Len Bergantino offers a different way of looking at psychology through a raw, uncensored view, which is both educational and entertaining. I recommend this book for its original style and provocative look at a much debated and discussed subject.

Pages: 492 | ASIN: B07KPZ5GDV

Xlibris

DENIAL OF REVERSE RACISM IN AMERICA BY: DR. LEN BERGANTINO

CLICK THIS LINK BELOW TO BUY THE BOOK THE DENIAL OF REVERSE

RACISM IN AMERICA FROM XLIBRIS

https://www.xlibris.com/en/bookstore/bookdetails/810739- thedenialof-reverse-racism-inamerica

CLICK THIS LINK BELOW TO BUY THE BOOK THE DENIAL OF REVERSE

RACISM IN AMERICA FROM Amazon

https://www.amazon.com/Denial-Reverse-Racism-America-New/dp/1955691460/ref=sr_1_1?crid=3GT68DOHQG7SA&keywords=Denial+of+reverse+racism&qid=1675789671&s=books&sprefix=denial+of+reverse+racism%2Cstripbooks-intl-ship%2C305&sr=1-1

CLICK THIS LINK BELOW TO BUY THE BOOK THE DENIAL OF REVERSE

RACISM IN AMERICA FROM Barnes&Noble

https://www.barnesandnoble.com/w/the-denial-of-reverse-racisminamerica-dr-lenbergantino-ed-dphd/1136653430?ean=9781796093902

THE ESSENCE OF MUSIC

Dr. Len Bergantino starts the book by giving a little background information about himself. He writes of when he was born and how his love for music started. Next, the author discusses his father, Dan Bergantino, and how he started him off reading music. Reading about Dr. Len Bergantino's early years was thrilling and gave one a sense of nostalgia. I enjoyed reading about his interaction with musical instruments, how different elements inspired him to love music, and how jolly he was. The first chapter of this book is cheerful and gets one excited about the rest of the book. Dr. Len Bergantino knows how to draw a reader to his art as he writes from his heart.

The Essence of Music: Musicality, Pure Sound, the Art of Melody, and Inner Peace is an intense collection of information in relation to music.

Why do people make music? How music influences the world, the author's relationship with music and lessons learned, the significance of making constructive music, and many more things. Dr. Len Bergantino has a backstory for almost everything he writes about. I applaud the author for his style of writing as it makes the reader understand how every instrument is special and why art is distinct to every individual. Music heals the soul and is also used to spread messages. Dr. Len Bergantino shares personal tales as he writes about his love for music. My favorite story from the author is about the night he was Sophia Loren's bodyguard. I enjoyed reading about that night's activities at the Italian Cultural Institute in 1996.

Dr. Len Bergantino is an excellent writer and is also a man of culture. It is remarkable how the author is knowledgeable and connected to his roots. Reading about Dr. Len Bergantino will inspire the reader to bond more with their traditions and appreciate where one comes from. His approach of using Caps in some sentences was attention-grabbing as it gets one to read in a different tone and also stresses the message he was to share.

This entertaining book reads like a mini autobiography for Dr. Len Bergantino. The major topic is music and its effects, but the parts that stick with readers are the personal tales shared by the author. You can never go a few pages without some comic relief as the author gets to be hilarious when talking about himself.
In *The Essence of Music*, you will learn about different musical instruments, how to play them and how crucial they all are. Through the author's story, you become exposed to different cultures and learn some complexities of life. This book is energizing to read and a great work of art when it comes to musicality. One of the major lessons you learn as a reader is that music has a healing component and the kind of music you listen to influences your perspective of life.

Pages: 286 | ASIN : B0876Q22FV

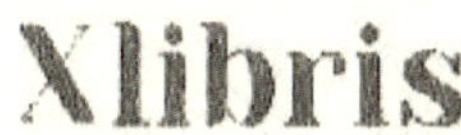
Xlibris

Germans – Jews – Holocausts and the Collective Unconscious

In *Germans Jews Holocausts and the Collective Unconscious*, Dr. Len Bergantino shares experiences in his life, telling personal stories and giving opinions on various issues in society. The author's method of storytelling is absorbing and entertaining. He writes from his heart, and writes objectively. When discussing controversial subjects, the author uses realistic examples to give his argument. As a reader, you feel enlightened and intrigued by the author's thoughts.

One of my favorite parts of the book was when the author discusses his background. I enjoyed reading about his professional life, family life and social life. His familiarity about different sectors and situations in life is laudable. *Germans Jews Holocausts and the Collective Unconscious* is for readers who are ready to expand their worldview. Dr. Len Bergantino addresses topics that may be considered taboo, and freely shares his views. The author sets precedence from the beginning of the book, and never loses track with the tone that he applies.

Every chapter is distinct, and the message being passed by the author is fascinating and edifying. Dr. Len Bergantino ensures that his readers get the full picture of things as he delves into each topic. The chapter on non-Germans and German Americans was exceptionally enlightening to me. In this chapter, the author compares modern Germans to Germans in the past, drawing comparisons and telling their differences. I learned that German Americans are a distinct group and, despite sharing heritage with Germans in Germany, they have peculiar mannerisms. The author also discusses Nazi history and the impact the holocaust has had on both Germans and Jews over the years. This chapter was especially enlightening because the author did not write what mainstream media reports. His discussions were genuine and involved real people he has met and interacted with.

History lovers will enjoy *Germans Jews Holocausts and the Collective Unconscious* because of the many historical events Dr. Len Bergantino covers. Topics that revolved around North American policies, current events, European policies, and the impact of war, media, and political alienations were my favorite. There is no defined method that the author uses when introducing new topics, which makes the book interesting to read. The author blends in a new story while narrating another story. He fuses two stories together, ensuring readers are engaged and always thinking about the information being shared. *Germans Jews Holocausts and the Collective Unconscious* discusses the realities that not many are aware of.

Pages: 264 | ASIN: B084KQ8FWZ

The Art of Psychotherapy and the Liberation of the Therapist

The Art of Psychotherapy and the Liberation of the Therapist is an academic work by Dr. Len Bergantino, Ed.D., Ph.D. This book educates the reader on psychotherapy and shows how it has progressed throughout the career of Dr. Bergantino as well as the work of many other experts whose work he has carefully studied and evaluated, and the experiences and views of the patients.

At the beginning of the book Dr. Bergantino points out that on the cover of his book is a picture of the American Revolutionary War hero Patrick Henry who was noted for his famous quote "Give me liberty or give me death." Dr. Bergantino explains that the only way to see progress in psychotherapy is if both the psychiatrist and the patient are completely liberated from everything around them and are entirely open and honest in the work that they are doing, and that is the approach he tried to use throughout his career.

This enlightening book is divided into two parts, with part two being a continuation and deeper dive into the topics in part one. This work covers topics from the existential moment, working with children, the holistic approach to psychotherapy, narcissism, couples therapy, schizophrenia, clinical psychology, and more. It also includes experts such as Freud, Whitaker, Frankl, and others. The book is filled with stories from Dr. Bergantino's career and shows readers how he handled situations with different patients such as a very tall, overweight man who carried a knife with him which made for a very unpleasant, unsafe, and stressful work environment, or a recent widower who was left alone with his young children, and many more.

A key term in this book is 'existential moment' which is defined as a full sense of being between patient and therapist. Those two human beings are capable of experiencing the focus of the moment, as it is applied to therapy. It deals with authenticity and the vulnerability that comes from two people facing each other as equals. Readers will also be met with the question that Shakespeare asked so many years ago, "To be or not to be?" The book explores how we interpret that question in our own lives, along with psychotherapy, and more interesting topics readers otherwise may not have thought about.

The Art Of Psychotherapy and the Liberation of the Therapist is an informative and thought-provoking book that I would recommend to readers looking for a compelling memoir or an edifying book on the topic of psychotherapy. This book takes an incredible dive into the world of psychotherapy and will appeal to practitioners, psychologists, or students in the psychotherapy field, as well as patients who want to learn more about psychotherapy.

Pages: 516 | ASIN: B07SKMW57C

Xlibris

The Sanctimonious Psychoproctological Invasions

In *The Sanctimonious Psychoproctological Invasions: The Handbook for Political Analysis*, Dr. Len Bergantino discusses the political climate in the United States while paying attention to the first amendment. The author extensively writes about this constitution clause, enlightening his readers on the political workings, how the government runs its daily business and the life the political class lives. The author exhausts every point regarding political discussions, giving sober analysis in every argument. The reader gets the privilege of reading through Dr. Bergantino's notes, letters, and opinions on issues that not many are comfortable discussing.

One of the most remarkable features of a good author is his bravado. Dr. Bergantino is bold in his work. He writes his truths and does not shy away from addressing controversial matters. The confidence displayed by the author makes reading this informative book interesting and engaging. Throughout the book, the reader learns about the political world and human stories. Dr. Len Bergantino shares personal tales, writing about his private life, professional life, passions, and the impact modern-day politics has had on his life. I relished reading his personal stories, his interactions with the who-is-who in the political class, and his contribution to his community.

Dr. Len Bergantino displays wisdom in his language and does not openly show partiality when writing about either Right Wing or Left Wing politics. The discussions are balanced, and the analysis is delivered objectively. Even when using strong language, Dr. Len Bergantino ensures that his message is not lost depending on the phrases he uses. America is the land of the free, and even with all its freedoms, American society seems to fall short in some areas. Dr. Len Bergantino does not conceal the evil of the political class, as he writes about it all; the good, the bad, the ugly, the embarrassing, and the pride instilled in Americans.

As an educator and political expert, Dr. Len Bergantino seems to be the ideal person to discuss the status quo and the battement of society. This educational book is arranged in an unconventional manner, which is great as the reader can choose and pick which topics to start reading first. The images of the author's works shared between the pages give the reader a good idea of how Dr. Len Bergantino's mind works and thus give one a better comprehension of these thoughts.

The Sanctimonious Psychoproctological Invasions: The Handbook for Political Analysis is a one-of-a-kind book that will expand readers' scope in politics, help readers to fully understand their rights as a citizen, and enlighten them on how the world works. I recommend this fascinating book to political science students and readers who enjoy political and socio-economic literature.

Pages: 366 | ISBN : 1955691835

POLITICAL PSYCHOLOGY INVASIONS

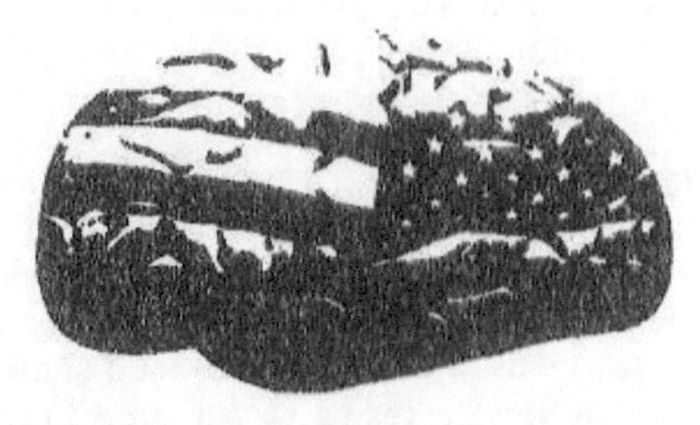

Dr. Len Bergantino starts this eye-opening book by taking the reader back to the 2020 election. He writes about the Democrat candidates at the time and analyzes Elizabeth Warren, Bernie Sanders, Kamala Harris, and Joe Biden. He then proceeds to write letters to President Trump, where he explains his aggravation and gives guidance on how certain issues should be handled. I take pleasure in reading Dr. Len Bergantino because of how raw he is. His language may come off as too strong, but the tone is what makes his writing distinct. Dr. Len Bergantino writes like a concerned citizen who wants to see his country run in a better manner.

Political Psychology Invasions looks at the past and current political situation and how today's events influence the future. In the book, readers learn about governance and how challenging it can be to contain some political elements. Dr.

Len Bergantino writes in an informative and authentic manner. He does not mind irritating some people as he is objective and true to his word. I like that the author gives praise where it's due and also criticizes when necessary. Dr. Len Bergantino analyzes the situations discussed in the book with impartiality and gives facts before concluding on a particular topic. In addition, the author explains the political class and how to perform your duties as a citizen.

Apart from the status quo, Dr. Len Bergantino also wrote about music and its role in society. Music may be a universal language, but to Dr. Len Bergantino, music is more than that. It is intimate to him as it is a family business. Being a professional psychoanalyst and a professional musician, Dr. Len Bergantino writes of how he is concerned by today's music. Having been introduced to music from a young age, Dr. Len Bergantino does not appreciate today's music as most of it is noise. Instead, the author writes about the importance of music among the masses and why musicians should improve. The author also advises on how to write better music as he narrates his experiences.

Amidst the political analysis and discussions, the author also writes of his adventures, travels, and life experiences. The fusing of his personal tales with the political talk was a great way of killing the monotony that may have been present. I like Dr. Len Bergantino because he writes with confidence. Even when calling out certain political figures, Dr. Len Bergantino gives a good reason. He is bright and great at analyzing human behavior and events.

Political Psychology Invasion will expose readers to politicians' dealings and help them better understand and examine future political events. This interesting book will give readers much to think over and help them better understand the political environment.

Pages: 178 | ASIN : B0876QCM35

Xlibris

Reverse Analysis, the Existential Shift, Gestalt Family Therapy and the Prevention of the Next Holocaust

In *Reverse Analysis, The Existential shift, Gestalt Family Therapy and the Prevention of the Next Holocaust*, the reader gets to experience life through other people's experiences. The author writes about different life situations and encounters and adds tales of professionals and icons to convey his message. His book is about life, therapy, change in perspective, and the future.

Dr. Len Bergantino writes in detail about how exciting or boring life can be depending on an individual's path. He has interesting takes and ideal examples that make the reading engrossing. This interesting book is generally about life, how we relate with other people, how our thoughts affect us, and improving the life we live. The author ensures that the reader understands every unfamiliar terminology and theory by fully explaining things. Dr. Len Bergantino is an excellent author because he knows how to blend casual discussion with academic and professional text. He will write about scientific and expert opinions and add a bit of a casual story to balance the discussion. I appreciate the author for being candid and nonpartisan, even when discussing sensitive issues. This book is a gem that will have you open your eyes to multiple problems in life. The author helps the reader connect with their conscious self and gets one to value every minute they are alive and functioning.

One of the things that you enjoy as a reader is the many stories the author shares. Dr. Len Bergantino writes well and understands the art of narration better than most. I especially loved reading his tales as he wrote about his professional and personal life. In every story, the reader gets a life lesson or prudent sayings. Dr. Len Bergantino is open and discusses his high and low moments without concealing crucial information. This book teaches you the definition of therapy and psychotherapy and how various therapists identify with the subject. The author also shares essential information about gestalt therapy.

Reverse Analysis, The Existential shift, Gestalt Family Therapy and the Prevention of the Next Holocaust has a dozen subjects that can help one improve their lifestyle. Dr. Len Bergantino uses notes from experts to expound on his concepts, which is an excellent idea as one gets multiple angles from other people. The book's arrangement is a tad unconventional but still easy to follow. The notes are brief but contain a critical message. One thing I love about Dr. Len Bergantino is how shrewd he is. Every topic discussed is well-researched, and the author considers expert opinion before analyzing.
I rate *Reverse Analysis, The Existential shift, Gestalt Family Therapy and the Prevention of the Next Holocaust* with 4 out of 5 stars for the excellent penmanship and for the advice that will make the reader an all-rounded better individual.

Pages: 246 | ASIN : B07QNSKBL2

When Baseball Was King the New York Yankees Were King of Baseball
First Review

When Baseball was King The New York Yankees were King of Baseball recounts some of the greatest baseball players ever. Author *Dr. Len Bergantino* is able to recount many of their stats, from how fast pitchers could throw and how fast the greatest players could hit! From Mickey Mantle, Yogi Berra, and Jackie Robinsons, we get to read about how great each player was. While mostly discussing great Yankee players, *Dr. Bergantino* also discusses some of the other great players from other teams, such as the Cleveland Indians and the Brooklyn Dodgers.

I enjoyed reading about some of baseball's greatest players in this enlightening book. The author is correct about baseball not being such a loved sport anymore. Most people seem to enjoy football now. While

I have personally heard about most of the players mentioned, I didn't know their stats. Reading about the batting averages from back then compared to the players now was eye-opening. It makes me wonder what has changed in the players between then and now.

I enjoyed reading the letters that *Dr. Bergantino* wrote to Carl Erskine. It was nice to see that Mr. Erskine replied to his letters as well. He even sent a copy of his book. While he originally disliked Carl Erskine because he was a great pitcher for the Dodgers, he realized he did like him in the end because he was such a great player.

There are scans of other books that *Dr. Len Bergantino* wrote inside this book. There are excerpts from those books as well. They are printed multiple times as well leaving the actual story to be about 45 pages. The rest is from the other books.

This is an illuminating book that conjures a nostalgic feeling while providing readers with interesting facts about great baseball players. I enjoyed this story, especially when the author talked about watching baseball as a kid. This is a great read for any fan of the New York Yankees and anyone interested in baseball history.

Pages: 98 | ASIN: B085WMX5P6

Xlibris

When Baseball Was King the New York Yankees Were King of Baseball
2nd Review

When Baseball Was King, The New York Yankees Were Kings of Baseball by Dr. Len Bergantino is the full recounted story of the popular sport and its greatest players. From baseball's history to its player's stats and respective journeys throughout their careers. And while the main focus is the New York Yankees, there is also mention of other great teams and their players.

The peculiarity of this book is that it's visually graphic. It includes texts and images from other sources such as magazines and newspapers. This adds a unique touch to back up the author's quotes and citations. However, at times it seems like the author simply copied and pasted the pages of the books he thought relevant without summarizing and citing the information correctly.

The book is fifty-three pages, almost a third of these being scans or excerpts from other books.

The story is narrated through Dr. Bergantino's point of view as he discovers baseball and dives further deeper into its history and greatest stars. He tells the story of how his father introduced him to the sport and how he then fell in love with it; this gives it a nostalgic touch that I'm sure old baseball fans will very much appreciate.

While this book is non-fiction and primarily informative, having a "character" narrate gives it a storylike quality that makes it more enjoyable and feels less of an educational text and more like something to read for fun. This book gives readers a general insight into the sport and exciting facts about the most prominent players. It's perfect for any baseball fans or as an introduction for anyone looking to get into the sport. It's short and easy to read and quickly captivates the reader's attention.

When Baseball Was King, The New York Yankees Were Kings of Baseball is an exciting historical look at the game with illuminating facts and entertaining stories.

Pages: 98 | ASIN : B085WMX5P6

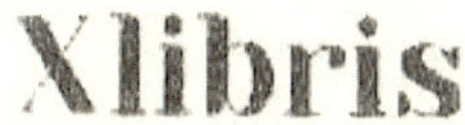

Xlibris

The Greatest Basketball Player I Ever Saw

Dr. Len Bergantino, Ed.D., Ph.D.

The Greatest Basketball Player I Ever Saw by Dr. Len Bergantino is a touching mix of sports biography and autobiography. It is likely the most unique biography you'll ever have the pleasure of reading. Doctor Bergantino is an eccentric writer who has already written on various subjects. However, with this book, he has turned his hand to writing a sports biography. The strange part is he has chosen to write it about a sportsman you will never have heard of who died at the tender age of 18.

The book is a biography of Billy Finn, Bergantino's high school best friend who died in a car crash before he ever had a chance to become famous. Bergantino spends much of the book explaining why he thinks Finn was the best basketball player of all time. Finn's abilities are described as almost supernatural. This part of the book will likely appeal to anyone interested in basketball or amateur sports.

The book isn't just about Billy Finn, the sportsman, however. Instead, it is a monument to Finn, Bergantino's friend. I think this is the part of the book that will really appeal to most readers. Bergantino shares with us, the reader, touching anecdotes of what he and Finn got up to as young men. His love for his childhood friend, even 50 years after his passing, is evident and touching.

Bergantino's affection for Finn is almost infectious. The book is written in such a way that the reader finds themselves caring about a young man they had never heard of before. Finn's personality is described as warts and all. The two young men don't always see eye to eye, and Bergantino doesn't shy away from this. Even the best of friends annoy each other from time to time.

The book is a short, easy read. Bergantino's writing is energetic if a bit frantic at times. He is a fan of hyperbole, and some of his claims about Finn may have to be taken with a pinch of salt. The eccentric style is enjoyable for most of the book, but the final chapter, in which he talks about how Finn has been reincarnated, may leave some readers, myself included, feeling a little cold. It feels like this last chapter goes off on a little bit of a tangent.

All in all, *The Greatest Basketball Player I Ever Saw* is a touching biography of a young man you more than likely have never heard of. But, whether you're a sports fan or not, the book is mostly a beautiful monument to a man whose best friend still bitterly misses him.

Pages: 81 | ASIN : B0865X1P48

Xlibris